How to Solve the Mind–Body Problem

Nicholas Humphrey

IMPRINT ACADEMIC

ALSO OF INTEREST FROM IMPRINT ACADEMIC
Full details on: http://www.imprint.co.uk

Series Editor:
Professor J.A. Goguen, Computer Science, UCSD

Thomas Metzinger, ed.,
Conscious Experience

Francisco Varela and Jonathan Shear, ed.,
The View from Within:
First-person approaches to the study of consciousness

Shaun Gallagher and Jonathan Shear, ed.,
Models of the Self

Joseph A. Goguen, ed.,
Art and the Brain

Benjamin Libet, Anthony Freeman and J.K.B. Sutherland, ed.,
The Volitional Brain: Towards a neuroscience of free will

Rafael E. Núñez and Walter J. Freeman, ed.,
Reclaiming Cognition: The primacy of action, intention and emotion

Leonard D. Katz, ed.,
Evolutionary Origins of Morality: Cross-disciplinary perspectives

Published in the UK by Imprint Academic
PO Box 200, Exeter EX5 5HY, UK

Published in the USA by Imprint Academic
Philosophy Documentation Center
PO Box 7147, Charlottesville, VA 22906-7147, USA

ISBN 0 907845 08 8 (paperback)

ISSN 1355 8250 (*Journal of Consciousness Studies*, **7**, No.4, 2000)

British Library Cataloguing in Publication Data
A catalogue record for this book is available from the British Library
Library of Congress Card Number : 00–101880

Cover illustration: Claire Harper

Contents

Contributors

Principal Author

Nicholas Humphrey,
Centre for Philosophy of the Natural and Social Sciences,
London School of Economics, Houghton Street, London WC2A 2AE, UK

Commentators

Andy Clark, Dept of Philosophy, Washington University,
Campus 1073, St Louis, MO 63130-4899, USA

Daniel Dennett, Center for Cognitive Studies, Tufts University,
520 Boston Avenue, Medford, MA 02155-5555, USA

Naomi Eilan, Dept. of Philosophy, University of Warwick,
Coventry, CV4 7AL, UK

Ralph Ellis, PO Box 81, Clarke Atlanta University,
James P. Brawley Drive at Fair Street SW, Atlanta, GA 30314, USA

Valerie Gray Hardcastle, Dept. of Philosophy, Virginia Polytechnic Institute
and State University, Blacksburg, VA 24061-0126, USA

Stevan Harnad, Dept. of Electronics and Computer Science,
University of Southampton, Highfield, Southampton, SO17 1BJ, UK

Natika Newton,
15 Cedar Lane, Setauket, NY 11733, USA

Christian de Quincey, Institute of Noetic Sciences
475 Gate Five Road, Suite 300, Sausalito, CA 94965-2835, USA

Carol Rovane, Dept. of Philosophy, Columbia University,
Morningside Heights, New York, NY 10027, USA

Robert Van Gulick, Dept. of Philosophy/Cognitive Science,
Syracuse University, Syracuse, NY 13244-117, USA

Nicholas Humphrey

How to Solve the Mind–Body Problem

Two hundred and fifty years ago Denis Diderot, commenting on what makes a great natural philosopher, wrote:

> They have watched the operations of nature so often and so closely that they are able to guess what course she is likely to take, and that with a fair degree of accuracy, even when they take it into their heads to provoke her with the most outlandish experiments. So that the most important service they can render to [others] . . . is to pass on to them that spirit of divination by means of which it is possible to *smell out*, so to speak, methods that are still to be discovered, new experiments, unknown results (Diderot, 1754, XXX, p. 66).

Whether Diderot would have claimed such a faculty in his own case is not made clear. But I think there is no question we should claim it for him. For, again and again, Diderot made astonishingly prescient comments about the future course of natural science. Not least, this:

> Just as in mathematics, all the properties of a curve turn out upon examination to be all the same property, but seen from different aspects, so in nature, when experimental science is more advanced, we shall come to see that all phenomena, whether of weight, elasticity, attraction, magnetism or electricity, are all merely aspects of a single state (Diderot, 1754, XLV, p. 68).

Admittedly the grand unifying theory that Diderot looked forward to has not yet been constructed. And contemporary physicists are still uncertain whether such a theory of *everything* is possible even in principle. But, within the narrower field that constitutes the study of *mind* and *brain*, cognitive scientists are increasingly confident of its being possible to have a unifying theory of these *two* things.

They — we — all assume that the human mind and brain are, as Diderot anticipated, aspects of a single state — a single state, in fact, of the material world, which could in principle be fully described in terms of its microphysical components. We assume that each and every instance of a human mental state is *identical* to a brain state, **mental state, m = brain state, b,** meaning that the mental state and the brain state pick out the same thing at this microphysical level. And usually we further assume that the nature of this identity is such that each type of mental state is multiply realizable, meaning that instances of this one type can be identical to instances of several different types of brain states that happen to be functionally equivalent.

Journal of Consciousness Studies, **7**, No. 4, 2000, pp. 5–20

What's more, we have reason to be confident that these assumptions are factually correct. For, as experimental science grows more advanced, we are indeed coming to see that mind and brain are merely aspects of a single state. In particular, brain-imaging studies, appearing almost daily in the scientific journals, demonstrate in ever more detail how specific kinds of mental activity (as reported by a mindful subject) are precisely correlated with specific patterns of brain activity (as recorded by external instruments). *This* bit of the brain lights up when a man is in pain, *this* when he conjures up a visual image, *this* when he tries to remember which day of the week it is, and so on.

No doubt many of us would say we have known all along that such correspondences must in principle exist. So that our faith in mind–brain identity hardly needs these technicolour demonstrations. Even so, it is, to say the least, both satisfying and reassuring to see the statistical facts of the identity being established, as it were, right before our eyes.

Yet it's one thing to see *that* mind and brain are aspects of a single state, but quite another to see *why* they are. It's one thing to be convinced by the statistics, but another to understand — as surely we all eventually want to — the causal or logical principles involved. Even while we have all the evidence required for *inductive generalization*, we may still have no basis for *deductive explanation*.

Let's suppose, by analogy, that we were to come to see, through a series of 'atmospheric-imaging' experiments, that whenever there is a visible shaft of lightning in the air there is a corresponding electrical discharge. We might soon be confident that the lightning and the electrical discharge are aspects of one and the same thing, and we should certainly be able to predict the occurrence of lightning whenever there is the electrical discharge. Even so, we might still have not a clue about what *makes* an electrical discharge manifest also as lightning.

Likewise, we might one day have collected so much detailed information about mind–brain correlations that we can predict which mental state will supervene on any specific brain state. Even so we might still have no idea as to the reasons why this brain state yields this mental state, and hence no way of deducing one from the other *a priori*.

But with lightning there could be — and of course historically there was — a way to progress to the next stage. The physico-chemical causes that underlie the identity could be discovered through further experimental research and new theorizing. Now the question is whether the same strategy will work for mind and brain.

When experimental science is even more advanced, shall we come to see not only *that* mind and brain are merely aspects of a single state, but *why* they have to be so? Indeed, shall we be able to see how an identity that might otherwise appear to be mysteriously contingent is in fact transparently necessary?

A few philosophers believe the answer must be No. Or, at any rate, they believe we shall never achieve this level of understanding for every single feature of the mind and brain. They would point out that not all identities are in fact open to analysis in logical or causal terms, even in principle. Some identities are metaphysically primitive, and have simply to be taken as givens. And quite possibly some basic features of the mind are in this class. David Chalmers, for example, takes this stance when he argues for a version of epiphenomenal dualism in which consciousness just happens to be a fundamental, non-derivative, property of matter (Chalmers, 1996).

But even supposing — as most people do — that all the *interesting* identities *are* in fact analysable in principle, it might still be argued that not all of them will be open to analysis by us human beings. Thus Colin McGinn believes that the reason why a full understanding of the mind–brain identity will never be achieved is not because the task is logically impossible but because there are certain kinds of understanding — and this is clearly one of them — which must for ever lie beyond our intellectual reach: no matter how much more factual knowledge we accumulate about mind and brain, we simply do not have what it would take to come up with the right theory (McGinn, 1989).

The poet Goethe, much earlier, counselled against what he considered to be the hubris of our believing that we humans can in fact solve every problem. 'In Nature', he said, 'there is an accessible element and an inaccessible. . . .

> Anyone who does not appreciate this distinction may wrestle with the inaccessible for a lifetime without ever coming near to the truth. He who does recognize it and is sensible will keep to the accessible and by progress in every direction within a field and consolidation, may even be able to wrest something from the inaccessible along the way — though here he will in the end have to admit that some things can only be grasped up to a certain point, and that Nature always retains behind her something problematic which it is impossible to fathom with our inadequate human faculties (Goethe, 1827).

It is not yet clear how far — if at all — such warnings should be taken seriously. Diderot, for one, would have advised us to ignore them. Indeed Diderot, ever the scientific modernist, regarded any claim by philosophers to have found limits to our understanding, and thus to set up No-Go areas, as an invitation to science (or experimental philosophy) to prove such rationalist philosophy wrong.

> Experimental philosophy knows neither what will come nor what will not come out of its labours; but it works on without relaxing. The philosophy based on reasoning, on the contrary, weighs possibilities, makes a pronouncement and stops short. It boldly said: 'light cannot be decomposed': experimental philosophy heard, and held its tongue in its presence for whole centuries; then suddenly it produced the prism, and said, 'light can be decomposed' (Diderot, 1754, XXIII, p. 46).

The hope now of cognitive scientists is of course that there is a prism awaiting discovery that will do for the mind–brain identity what Newton's prism did for light — a prism that will again send the philosophical doubters packing.

I am with them in this hope. But I am also concerned that we should not block our ears to the philosophical warnings entirely. For there is no question that the likes of McGinn and Goethe might have a point. Indeed, I'd say they might have more than a point: they will actually become right by default, *unless and until we can set out the identity in a way that meets certain minimum standards for explanatory possibility.*

To be precise, we need to recognize that there can be no hope of scientific progress so long as we continue to write down the identity in such a way that the mind terms and the brain terms are patently *incommensurable* (cf. the discussion of the same problem by Kelso, 1995, p. 29). The problem will be especially obvious if the *dimensions* do not match up.

I use the word 'dimensions' here advisedly. When we do physics at school we are taught that the 'physical dimensions' of each side of an equation must be the same. If one side has the dimensions of a volume, the other side must be a volume too, and it cannot be, for example, an acceleration; if one side has the dimensions of power, the

other side must be power too and it cannot be momentum; and so on. As Frank
Ramsey put this in his classical *Dynamics* textbook: 'The consideration of dimensions is a useful check in dynamical work, for each side of an equation must represent
the same physical thing and therefore must be of the same dimensions in mass [**m**],
space [**s**] and time [**t**]' (Ramsey, 1954, p. 42).

Indeed so strong a constraint is this that, as Ramsey went on, 'sometimes a consideration of dimensions alone is sufficient to determine the form of the answer to a
problem.' For example, suppose we want to know the form of the equation that
relates the energy contained in a lump of matter, **E**, to its mass, **M**, and the velocity of
light, **C**. Since **E** can only have the dimension $\mathbf{ms^2t^{-2}}$, **M** the dimension **m** and **C** the
dimension $\mathbf{st^{-1}}$, we can conclude without further ado that the equation must have the
form $\mathbf{E = MC^2}$. By the same token, if anyone were to propose instead that
$\mathbf{E = MC^3}$, we would know immediately that something was wrong.

But what is true of these dynamical equations is of course just as true of all other
kinds of identity equations. We can be sure in advance that, if any proposed identity
is to have even a chance of being valid, both sides must represent the same *kind* of
thing. Indeed we can generalize this beyond physical dimensions, to say that both
sides must have the same conceptual dimensions, which is to say they must belong to
the same generic class.

So, if it is suggested for example that Mark Twain and Samuel Clemens are identical, **Mark Twain = Samuel Clemens**, we can believe it because both sides of the
equation are in fact people. Or, if it is suggested that Midsummer Day and 21st June
are identical, **Midsummer Day = 21st June**, we can believe it because both sides
are days of the year. But were someone to suggest that Mark Twain and Midsummer
Day are identical, **Mark Twain = Midsummer Day**, we should know immediately
this equation is a false one.

Now, to return to the mind–brain identity: when the proposal is that a certain mental state is identical to a certain brain state, **mental state, *m* = brain state, *b***, the
question is: do the dimensions of the two sides match?

The answer surely is, Yes, sometimes they do, or at any rate they can be made to.

Provided cognitive science delivers on its promise, it should soon be possible to
characterize many mental states in computational or functional terms, i.e. in terms of
rules connecting inputs to outputs. But brain states too can relatively easily be
described in these same terms. So it should then be quite straightforward, in principle, to get the two sides of the equation to line up.

Most of the states of interest to psychologists — states of remembering, perceiving, wanting, talking, thinking, and so on — are in fact likely to be amenable to this
kind of functional analysis. So, although it is true there is still a long way to go before
we can claim much success in practice, at least the research strategy is clear.

We do an experiment, say, in which we get subjects to recall what day of the week
it is, and at the same time we record their brain activity by MRI. We discover that
whenever a person thinks to himself 'today is Tuesday', a particular area of the brain
lights up. We postulate the identity: **recalling that today is Tuesday = activity of
neurons in the calendula nucleus**.

We then try, on the one hand, to provide a computational account of what is
involved in this act of recalling the day; and, on the other hand, we examine the local

brain activity and try to work out just what is being computed. Hopefully, when the results are in, it all matches nicely. A clear case of **Mark Twain = Samuel Clemens**.

But of course cases like this are notoriously the 'easy' cases — and they are not the ones that most philosophers are really fussed about. The 'hard' cases are precisely those where it seems that this kind of functional analysis is not likely to be possible. And this means especially those cases that involve *phenomenal consciousness*: the subjective sensation of redness, the taste of cheese, the pain of a headache, and so on. These are the mental states that Isaac Newton dubbed sensory 'phantasms' (Munz, 1997), and which are now more generally (although often less appropriately) spoken of as 'qualia'.

The difficulty in these latter cases is not that we cannot establish the factual evidence for the identity. Indeed this part of the task may be just as easy as in the case of cognitive states such as remembering the day. We do an experiment, say, in which we get subjects to experience colour sensations, while again we examine their brain by MRI. We discover that whenever someone has a red sensation, there is activity in cortical area Q6. So we postulate the identity: **phantasm of red = activity in Q6 cortex**.

So far, so good. But it is the next step that is problematical. For now, if we try the same strategy as before and attempt to provide a functional description of the phantasm so as to be able to match it with a functional description of the brain state, the way is barred. No one it seems has the least idea how to characterize the phenomenal experience of redness in functional terms — or for that matter how to do it for any other variety of sensory phantasm. And in fact there are well-known arguments (such as the Inverted Spectrum) that purport to prove that it cannot be done, even in principle.

If not a functional description, then, might there be some other way of describing these elusive states, which being also applicable to brain states, could save the day? Unfortunately, the philosophical consensus seems to be that the answer must be No. For many philosophers seem to be persuaded that phenomenal states and brain states are indeed essentially such different kinds of entity that there is simply no room whatever for negotiation. Colin McGinn, in a fantasy dialogue, expressed the plain hopelessness of it sharply: 'Isn't it perfectly evident to you that [the brain] is just the wrong kind of thing to give birth to [phenomenal] consciousness. You might as well assert that numbers emerge from biscuits or ethics from rhubarb' (McGinn, 1993). A case of **Mark Twain = Midsummer Day**.

Yet, as we've seen, this will not do! At least not if we are still looking for explanatory understanding. So, where are we scientists to turn?

Let's focus on the candidate identity: **phantasm, p = brain state, b**. Given that the statistical evidence supporting it remains as strong as ever, there would seem to be three ways that we can go.

1. We can accept that, despite everything, this equation is in fact false. Whatever the statistical evidence for there being a correlation between the two, there is really *not* an identity between the two states. Indeed all the correlation shows is just that: that the states are *co-related*. And if we want to pursue it, we shall have then to go off and look for some other theoretical explanation for this correlation — God's whim, for instance. (This would have been Descartes' preferred solution.)

2. We can continue to believe in the equation, while at the same time we grudgingly acknowledge that we have met our match: either the identity does not have an explanation or else the explanation really is beyond our human reach. And, recognizing now that there is no point in pursuing it, we shall be able, with good conscience, to retire and do something else. (This is McGinn's preferred solution.)

3. We can doggedly insist both that the identity is real and that we shall explain it somehow — when eventually we do find the way of bringing the dimensions into line. But then, despite the apparent barriers, we shall have to set to work to brow-beat the terms on one side or other of the identity equation in such way as to *make* them line up. (This is my own and I hope a good many others' preferred solution.)

Now, if we do choose this third option, there are several possibilities.

One strategy would be to find a new way of conceiving of sensory phantasms so as to make them more obviously akin to brain states. But, let's be careful. We must not be *too* radical in redefining these phantasms or we shall be accused of redefining away the essential point. Daniel Dennett's sallies in this direction can be a warning to us (Dennett, 1991). His suggestion that sensations are nothing other than complex behavioural (even purely linguistic?) dispositions, while defensible in his own terms, has proved too far removed from most people's intuitions to be persuasive.

An alternative strategy would be to find a new way of conceiving of brain states so as to make them more like sensory phantasms. But again we must not go too far. Roger Penrose is the offender this time (Penrose, 1989). His speculations about the brain as a quantum computer, however ingenious, have seemed to most neuroscientists to require too much special pleading to be taken seriously.

Or then again, there would be the option of doing *both*. My own view is that we should indeed try to meddle with both sides of the equation to bring them into line. Dennett expects all the compromise to come from the behavioural psychology of sensation, Penrose expects it all to come from the physics of brain states. Neither of these strategies seems likely to deliver what we want. But it's amazing how much more promising things look when we allow some give on *both* sides — when we attempt to adjust our concept of sensory phantasms *and* our concept of brain states until they do match up.

So, *this*, I suppose, is how to solve the mind–brain problem. We shall need to work on both sides to define the relevant mental states and brain states in terms of concepts that really do have *dual currency* — being equally applicable to the mental and the material. . . . And now all that remains, for this paper, is to do it.

Then, let's begin. **Phantasm, p = brain state, b**. Newton himself wrote: 'To determine . . . by what modes or actions light produceth in our minds the phantasms of colours is not so easy. And I shall not mingle conjectures with certainties' (Newton, 1671, p. 3085). Three and a half centuries later, let us see if we can at least mix some certainties with the conjectures.

First, on one side of the equation, these sensory phantasms. Precisely what are we are talking about here? What kind of thing are they? What indeed are their dimensions?

Philosophers are — or at any rate have become in recent years — remarkably cava-lier about the need for careful definition in this area. They bandy about terms such as 'phenomenal properties', 'what it's like', 'conscious feelings', and so on, to refer to whatever it is that is at issue when people point inwardly to their sensory experience — as if the hard-won lessons of positivist philosophy had never been learned. In par-ticular that over-worked term 'qualia', which did at least once have the merit of meaning something precise (even if possibly vacuous, see Dennett, 1988), is now widely used as a catch-all term for anything vaguely subjective and qualitative.

It is no wonder, then, that working scientists, having been abandoned by those who might have been their pilots, have tended to lose their way even more comprehen-sively. Francis Crick and Christoph Koch (1999), for example, begin a recent paper by saying that 'everyone has a rough idea of what is meant by consciousness' and that 'it is better to avoid a precise definition of consciousness'. In the same vein Susan Greenfield (1998, p. 210) writes 'consciousness is impossible to define . . . perhaps then it is simply best to give a hazy description, something like consciousness being "your first-person, personal world".' While Antonio Damasio (2000, p. 9) is fuzzier still: 'Quite candidly, this first problem of consciousness is the problem of how we get a "movie in the brain". . . the fundamental components of the images in the movie metaphor are thus made of qualia.'

But this is bad. Hazy or imprecise descriptions can only be a recipe for trouble. And, anyway, they are unnecessary. For the fact is we have for a long time had the conceptual tools for seeing through the haze and distinguishing the phenomenon of central interest.

Try this. Look at a red screen, and consider what mental states you are experienc-ing. Now let the screen suddenly turn blue, and notice how things change. The impor-tant point to note is that there are *two* quite distinct parts to the experience, and *two* things that change.

First (and I mean first), there is a change in the experience of something happening to yourself — the bodily sensation of the quality of light arriving at your eye. Second, there is a change in your attitude towards something in the outer world — your perception of the colour of an external object.

It was Thomas Reid, genius of the Scottish enlightenment, who over two hundred years ago first drew philosophical attention to the remarkable fact that we human beings — and presumably many other animals also — do in fact use our senses in these two quite different ways:

> The external senses have a double province — to make us feel, and to make us perceive. They furnish us with a variety of sensations, some pleasant, others painful, and others indifferent; at the same time they give us a conception and an invincible belief of the exis-tence of external objects. . . .

> Sensation, taken by itself, implies neither the conception nor belief of any external object. It supposes a sentient being, and a certain manner in which that being is affected; but it supposes no more. Perception implies a conviction and belief of something external — something different both from the mind that perceives, and the act of perception. Things so different in their nature ought to be distinguished (Reid, 1785, II, Ch. 17 & 16).

For example, Reid said, we smell a rose, and two separate and parallel things hap-pen: we both feel the sweet smell at our own nostrils and we perceive the external presence of a rose. Or, again, we hear a hooter blowing from the valley below: we both feel the booming sound at our own ears and we perceive the external presence of a ship down in the Firth. In general we can and usually do use the evidence of sensory stimulation *both* to provide a 'subject-centred affect-laden representation of what's happening to me', *and* to provide 'an objective, affectively neutral representation of what's happening out there' (Humphrey, 1992).

Now it seems quite clear that what we are after when we try to distinguish and define the realm of sensory phantasms is the first of these: sensation rather than perception. Yet one reason why we find it so hard to do the job properly is that it is so easy to muddle the two up. Reid again:

> [Yet] the perception and its corresponding sensation are produced at the same time. In our experience we never find them disjoined. Hence, we are led to consider them as one thing, to give them one name, and to confound their different attributes. It becomes very difficult to separate them in thought, to attend to each by itself, and to attribute nothing to it which belongs to the other. To do this, requires a degree of attention to what passes in our own minds, and a talent for distinguishing things that differ, which is not to be expected in the vulgar, and is even rarely found in philosophers. . . .

> I shall conclude this chapter by observing that, as the confounding our sensations with that perception of external objects which is constantly conjoined with them, has been the occasion of most of the errors and false theories of philosophers with regard to the senses; so the distinguishing these operations seems to me to be the key that leads to a right understanding of both (Reid, 1785, II, Ch. 17 & 16).

To repeat: sensation has to do with the self, with bodily stimulation, with feelings about what's happening *now* to *me* and how *I* feel about it; perception by contrast has to do with judgements about the objective facts of the external world. Things so different in their nature *ought* to be distinguished. Yet rarely are they. Indeed many people still assume that perceptual judgements and even beliefs, desires and thoughts can have a pseudo-sensory phenomenology in their own right.

Philosophers will be found claiming for example that 'there is something it is like' not only to have sensations such as feeling warmth on one's skin, but also to have perceptions such as seeing the shape of a distant cube, and even to hold propositional attitudes such as believing that Paris is the capital of France (Block, 1995; Searle 1992; see also my discussion in Humphrey, 1999b). Meanwhile psychologists, adopting a half-understood vocabulary borrowed from philosophy, talk all too casually about such hybrid notions as the perception of 'dog qualia' on looking at a picture of a dog (Ramachandran and Hirstein, 1997). While these category mistakes persist we might as well give up.

So this must be the first step: we have to mark off the phenomenon that interests us — sensation — and get the boundary *in the right place*. But then the real work of analysis begins. For we must home in on what *kind of thing* we are dealing with.

Look at the red screen. You feel the red sensation. You perceive the red screen. We do in fact talk of both sensation and perception in structurally similar ways. We talk of *feeling* or *having* sensations — as if somehow these sensations, like perceptions, were the *objects* of our sensing, sense *data*, out there waiting for us to grasp them or observe them with our mind's eye.

But, as Reid long ago recognized, our language misleads us here. In truth, sensations are no more the objects of sensing than, say, volitions are the objects of willing, intentions the objects of intending, or thoughts the object of thinking.

Thus, *I feel a pain; I see a tree*: the first denoteth a sensation, the last a perception. The grammatical analysis of both expressions is the same: for both consist of an active verb and an object. But, if we attend to the things signified by these expressions, we shall find that, in the first, the distinction between the act and the object is not real but grammatical; in the second, the distinction is not only grammatical but real.

The form of the expression, *I feel pain*, might seem to imply that the feeling is something distinct from the pain felt; yet in reality, there is no distinction. As *thinking a thought* is an expression which could signify no more than *thinking*, so *feeling a pain* signifies no more than *being pained*. What we have said of pain is applicable to every other mere sensation (Reid, 1764, p. 112).

So sensory awareness is an activity. We do not have pains we get to be pained.

This is an extraordinarily sophisticated insight. And all the more remarkable that Reid should have come to it two hundred years before Wittgenstein was tearing his hair about similar problems and not getting noticeably further forward.

Even so, I believe Reid himself got only part way to the truth here. For my own view (developed in detail in my book, *A History of the Mind*, 1992) is that the right expression is not so much 'being pained' as 'paining'. That is to say, sensing is not a passive state at all, but rather a form of active engagement with the stimulus occurring at the body surface.

When, for example, I feel pain in my hand, or taste salt on my tongue, or equally when I have a red sensation at my eye, I am not *being* pained, or *being* stimulated saltily, or *being* stimulated redly. In each case I am in fact the active agent. I am not sitting there passively absorbing what comes in *from* the body surface, I am reflexly reaching out *to* the body surface with an evaluative response — a response appropriate to the stimulus and the body part affected.

Furthermore, it is this *efferent activity* that I am aware of. So that what I actually experience as the feeling — the sensation of what is happening to me — is my reading of my own response to it. Hence the quality of the experience, the way it feels, instead of revealing the way something is being done *to* me, reveals the very way something is being done *by* me.

- *This* is how I feel about what's happening right now at my hand — I'm feeling painily about it!
- *This* is how I feel about what's happening right now at this part of the field of my eye — I'm feeling redly about it!

In my book I proposed that we should call the activity of sensing 'sentition'. The term has not caught on. But I bring it up again here, in passing, because I believe we can well do with a word that captures the active nature of sensation: and sentition, resonating as it does with volition and cognition, sounds the right note of directed self-involvement.

The idea, to say it again, is that this sentition involves the subject 'reaching out to the body surface with an evaluative response — a response appropriate to the stimulus and the body part affected'. This should not of course be taken to imply that such sensory responses actually result in overt bodily behaviour — at least certainly not in human beings as we are now. Nonetheless I think there is good reason to suppose that the responses we make today have in fact *evolved* from responses that in the past did carry through into actual behaviour. And the result is that even today the experience of sensation retains many of the original characteristics of the experience of true bodily action.

Let's consider, for example, the following five defining properties of the experience of sensation — and, in each case, let's compare an example of sensing, *feeling a pain in my hand*, with an example of bodily action, *performing a hand wave*.

1. **Ownership**. Sensation always *belongs to the subject*. When I have the pain in my hand, I *own* the paining, it's mine and no one else's, I am the one and only *author* of it — as when I wave my hand, I *own and am the author of* the action of waving.

2. **Bodily location**. Sensation is always *indexical* and *invokes a particular part of the subject's body*. When I have the pain in my hand, the paining intrinsically involves *this* part of *me* — as when I wave my hand the waving too intrinsically involves *this* part of *me*.

3. **Presentness**. Sensation is always *present tense, ongoing and imperfect*. When I have the pain in my hand, the paining is in existence just *now for the time being* — as when I wave my hand the waving too exists just *now*.

4. **Qualitative modality**. Sensation always has the feel of one of several *qualitatively distinct modalities*. When I have the pain in my hand, the paining belongs to the class of *somatic* sensations, quite different in their whole style from, say, the class of visual sensations or of olfactory ones — as when I wave my hand the waving belongs to the class of *hand-waves*, quite different in style from other classes of bodily actions such as, say, the class of face-smiles or of knee-jerks.

5. **Phenomenal immediacy**. Most important, sensation is always *phenomenally immediate*, and the four properties above are *self-disclosing*. Thus, when I have the pain in my hand my impression is simply that *my hand hurts*: and, when my hand hurts, the fact that it is *my* hand (rather than someone else's), that it is my *hand* (rather than some other bit of me), that it is hurting *now* (rather than some other time), and that it is acting in a *painful* fashion (rather than acting in a visual, gustatory or auditory fashion), are facts of which I am directly and immediately aware *for the very reason that it is I, the author of the paining, who make these facts* — just as when I wave my hand, my impression is simply that my hand waves, and all the corresponding properties of this action too are facts of which I, *the author of the wave*, am immediately aware for similar reasons.

Thus, in these ways, and others that I could point to, the positive analogies between sensations and bodily activities add up. And yet, I acknowledge right away that there is also an obvious disanalogy: namely that, to revert to that old phrase, it is 'like something' to have sensations, but not like anything much to engage in most other bodily activities!

To say the least, our experience of other bodily activities is usually very much shallower. When I wave my hand there may be, perhaps, the ghost of some phenomenal experience. But surely what it's like to wave hardly compares with what it's like to feel pain, or taste salt or sense red. The bodily activity comes across as a flat and papery phenomenon, whereas the sensation seems so much more velvety and thick. The bodily activity is like an unvoiced whisper, whereas the sensation is like the rich *self-confirming* sound of a piano with the sustaining pedal down.

Of course neither metaphor quite captures the difference in quality I am alluding to. But still I think the sustaining pedal brings us surprisingly close. For I believe that ultimately the key to an experience being 'like something' does in fact lie in the experience *being like itself in time* — hence *being about itself,* or *taking itself as its own intentional object.* And this is achieved, in the special case of sensory responses, through a kind of *self-resonance* that effectively stretches out the present moment to create what I have called the *thick moment of consciousness* (Humphrey, 1995).

There are, of course, loose ends to this analysis and ambiguities. But I'd say there are surely fewer of both than we began with. And this is the time to take stock, and move on.

The task was to recast the terms on each side of the mind–brain identity equation, **phantasm,** p = **brain state,** b, so as to make them look more like each other.

What we have done so far is to redescribe the left hand side of the equation in progressively more concrete terms. Thus the phantasm of pain becomes the sensation of pain, the sensation of pain becomes the experience of actively paining, the activity of paining becomes the activity of reaching out to the body surface in a painy way, and this activity becomes self-resonant and thick. . . . And with each step we have surely come a little closer to specifying something of a *kind* that we can get a handle on.

We can therefore turn our attention to the right hand side of the equation. As Ramsey wrote, 'Sometimes a consideration of dimensions alone is sufficient to determine the form of the answer to a problem.' If we now have this kind of thing on the mind side, we need to discover something like it on the brain side. If the mind term involves a state of *actively doing something about something*, namely issuing commands for an evaluative response addressed to body surface, then the brain term must also be a state of actively doing something about something, presumably doing the corresponding thing. If the mind term involves *self-resonance,* then the brain state must also involve self-resonance. And so on.

Is this still the impossibly tall-order that it seemed to be earlier — still a case of ethics on one side, rhubarb on the other? No, I submit that the hard problem has in fact been transformed into a relatively easy problem. For we are now dealing with something on the mind side that surely *could* have the same dimensions as a brain state *could*. Concepts such as 'indexicality', 'present-tenseness', 'modal quality' and 'authorship' are indeed dual currency concepts of just the kind required.

It looks surprisingly good. We can surely now imagine what it would take on the brain side to make the identity work. But I think there is double cause to be optimistic. For, as it turns out, this picture of what is needed on the brain side ties in beautifully with a plausible account of the evolution of sensations.

I shall round off this paper by sketching in this evolutionary history. And if I do it in what amounts to cartoon form, I trust this will at least be sufficient to let the major themes come through.

Let's return, then, in imagination to the earliest of times and imagine a primitive amoeba-like animal floating in the ancient seas.

This animal has a defining edge to it, a structural boundary. This boundary is crucial: the animal *exists* within this boundary — everything within it is part of the animal, belongs to it, is part of 'self', everything outside it is part of 'other'. The boundary holds the animal's own substance in and the rest of the world out. The boundary is the vital frontier across which exchanges of material and energy and information can take place.

Now light falls on the animal, objects bump into it, pressure waves press against it, chemicals stick to it. No doubt some of these surface events are going to be a good thing for the animal, others bad. If it is to survive it must evolve the ability to sort out the good from the bad and to respond differently to them — reacting to this stimulus with an *ow!* to that with an *ouch!* to this with a *whowee!*

Thus, when, say, salt arrives at its skin it detects it and makes a characteristic wriggle of activity — it wriggles saltily. When red light falls on it, it makes a different kind of wriggle — it wriggles redly. These are adaptive responses, selected because they are appropriate to the animal's particular needs. Wriggling saltily has been selected as the best response to salt, while wriggling sugarly, for example, would be the best response to sugar. Wriggling redly has been selected as the best response to red light, while wriggling bluely would be the best response to blue light.

To begin with these wriggles are entirely local responses, organized immediately around the site of stimulation. But later there develops something more like a reflex arc passing via a central ganglion or proto-brain: information arrives from the skin, it gets assessed, and appropriate adaptive action is taken.

Still, as yet, these sensory responses are nothing other than responses, and there is no reason to suppose that the animal is in any way mentally aware of what is happening. Let's imagine however that, as this animal's life becomes more complex, the time comes when it will indeed be advantageous for it to have some kind of inner knowledge of what is affecting it, which it can begin to use as a basis for more sophisticated planning and decision making. So it needs the capacity to form *mental representations* of the sensory stimulation at the surface of its body and how it feels about it.

Now, one way of developing this capacity might be to start over again with a completely fresh analysis of the incoming information from the sense organs. But this would be to miss a trick. For, the fact is that all the requisite details about the stimulation — where the stimulus is occurring, what kind of stimulus it is, and how it should be dealt with — are already encoded in the command signals the animal is issuing when it makes the appropriate sensory response.

Hence, all the animal needs to do to represent the stimulation is to pick up on these already-occurring command signals. For example, to sense the presence of salt at a certain location on its skin, it need only monitor its own signals for wriggling saltily at that location, or, equally, to sense the presence of red light it need only monitor its signals for wriggling redly.

Note well, however, that all this time the animal's concern is merely with what's occurring at its body surface. By monitoring its own responses, it forms a representation of 'WHAT IS HAPPENING TO ME'. But, at this stage, the animal neither knows nor cares *where the stimulation comes from*, let alone what the stimulation may imply about the world *beyond* its body.

Yet wouldn't it be better off if it *were* to care about the world beyond? Let's say a pressure wave presses against its side — wouldn't it be better off if, besides being aware of feeling the pressure wave as such, it were able to interpret this stimulus as signalling an approaching predator? A chemical odour drifts across its skin — wouldn't it be better off if it were able to interpret this stimulus as signalling the presence of a tasty worm? In short, wouldn't the animal be better off if, as well as reading the stimulation at its body surface merely in terms of its immediate affective value, it were able to interpret it as a *sign* of 'WHAT IS HAPPENING OUT THERE'?

The answer of course is, Yes. And we can be sure that, early on, animals did in fact hit on the idea of using the information contained in body surface stimulation for this novel purpose — *perception* in addition to *sensation*. But the purpose was indeed *so* novel that it meant a very different style of information-processing was needed. When the question is 'what is happening to me?', the answer that is wanted is qualitative, present-tense, transient and subjective. When the question is 'what is happening out there?', the answer that is wanted is quantitative, analytical, permanent and objective.

So, to cut a long story short, there developed in consequence two parallel channels to subserve the very different readings we now make of an event at the surface of the body, sensation and perception: one providing an affect-laden modality-specific body-centred representation of what the stimulation is doing to me and how I feel about it, the other providing a more neutral, abstract, body-independent representation of the outside world.

Sensation and perception continued along relatively independent paths in evolution. But we need not be concerned further with perception in this paper. For it is the fate of sensation that matters to our story.

As we left it, the animal is actively responding to stimulation with public bodily activity, and its experience or proto-experience of sensation (if we can now call it that) arises from its monitoring its own command signals for these sensory responses. Significantly, these responses are still tied in to the animal's survival and their form is still being maintained by natural selection.

Yet, the story is by no means over. For, as this animal continues to evolve and to change its lifestyle, the nature of the selection pressures is bound to alter. In particular, as the animal becomes more independent of its immediate environment, it has less and less to gain from the responses it has always been making directly to the surface stimulus as such. In fact there comes a time when, for example, wriggling saltily or redly at the point of stimulation no longer has any adaptive value at all.

Then why not simply give up on this primitive kind of local responding altogether? The reason why not is that, even though the animal may no longer want to respond directly to the stimulation at its body surface as such, it still wants to be able to keep up to date mentally with what's occurring (not least because this level of sensory representation retains a crucial role in policing perception (see Humphrey, 1999a)). So, even though the animal may no longer have any use for the sensory responses in themselves, it has by this time become quite dependent on the secondary representational functions that these responses have acquired. And since the way it has been getting these representations in the past has been by monitoring its own command signals for sensory responses, it clearly cannot afford to stop issuing these command signals entirely.

So, the situation now is this. In order to be able to represent 'what's happening to me', the animal must in fact continue to issue commands such as *would* produce an appropriate response at the right place on the body *if* they were to carry through into bodily behaviour. But, given that the behaviour is no longer wanted, it may be better if these commands remain virtual or as-if commands — in other words, commands which, while retaining their original intentional properties, do not in fact have any real effects.

The upshot is — or so I've argued — that, over evolutionary time, there is a slow but remarkable change. What happens is that the whole sensory activity gets 'privatized': the command signals for sensory responses get short-circuited before they reach the body surface, so that instead of reaching all the way out to the site of stimulation they now reach only to points closer and closer in on the incoming sensory nerve, until eventually the whole process becomes closed off from the outside world in an internal loop within the brain (see Figure 1).

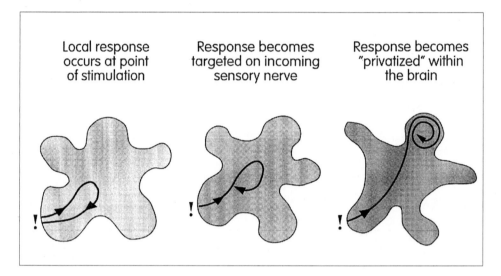

Figure 1

Now once *this* happens the role of natural selection must of course sharply diminish. The sensory responses have lost all their original biological importance and have in fact disappeared from view. Therefore selection is no longer involved in determining the form of these responses and *a fortiori* it can no longer be involved in determining the quality of the representations based on them.

But the fact is that this privacy has come about only at the very end, after natural selection has done its work to shape the sensory landscape. There is therefore every reason to suppose that the forms of sensory responses and the corresponding experiences have already been more or less permanently fixed. And although, once selection becomes irrelevant, these forms may be liable to drift somewhat, they are likely always to reflect their evolutionary pedigree. Thus responses that started their evolutionary life as dedicated wriggles of acceptance or rejection of a stimulus will still be recognizably of their kind right down to the present day.

Yet, something is not in place yet: the 'thickness factor'. And, as it happens, there is a further remarkable evolutionary development to come — made possible by the progressive shortening of the sensory response pathway.

It has been true all along, ever since the days when sensory responses were indeed actual wriggles at the body surface, that they have been having *feedback* effects by modifying the very stimulation to which they are a response. In the early days, how-ever, this feedback circuit was too round-about and slow to have had any interesting consequences. However, as and when the process becomes internalized and the cir-cuit so much shortened, the conditions are there for a significant degree of recursive interaction to come into play. That's to say, the command signals for sensory responses begin to loop back upon themselves, becoming in the process partly self-creating and self-sustaining. These signals still have to be initiated by input from the body surface, and still get styled by it, but they have also become signals about themselves.

To return to our identity equation: We *needed* a certain set of features on the brain side. We could have *invented* them if we were brave enough. But now, I submit, we actually have them *handed to us on a plate* by an evolutionary story that delivers on every important point.

I acknowledge that there is more to be done. And the final solution to the mind–body problem, if ever we do agree on it, may still look rather different from the way I'm telling it here. But the fact remains that this approach to the problem has to be the right one. There is no escaping the need for dual currency concepts — and any future theory will have to play by these rules.

Diderot wrote

> A tolerably clever man began his book with these words: '*Man, like all animals, is com-posed of two distinct substances, the soul and the body. If anyone denies this proposition it is not for him that I write.*' I nearly shut the book. Oh! ridiculous writer, if I once admit these two distinct substances, you have nothing more to teach me (Diderot, 1774, p. 139).

This paper has been about how to make one thing of these two.

Acknowledgment

I am grateful to have had financial support from Derek Goldsmith, through the Goldsmith Project, while working on this paper.

References

Block, N. (1995), 'On a confusion about a function of consciousness', *Behavioral and Brain Sci-ences*, **18**, pp. 227–47.
Chalmers, D.J. (1996), *The Conscious Mind* (Oxford: Oxford University Press).
Crick, F. & Koch, C. (1999), 'The unconscious homunculus', *Neuro-Psychoanalysis*, in press.
Damasio, A. (2000), *The Feeling of What Happens* (London: Heinemann).
Dennett, D.C. (1988), 'Quining Qualia', in *Consciousness in Contemporary Science*, ed. A.J. Marcel & E. Bisiach (Oxford: Clarendon Press).
Dennett, D.C. (1991), *Consciousness Explained* (New York: Little Brown).
Diderot, D. (1754/1982), *On the Interpretation of Nature*, in *The Irresistible Diderot*, ed. J.H. Mason (London: Quartet).
Diderot, D. (1774/1937), *Elements of Physiology*, in *Diderot: Interpreter of Nature*, ed. J.Kemp (London: Lawrence & Wishart).
Goethe, J.W. von (1827), *Conversations with Eckermann*, 11th April 1827.
Greenfield, S. (1998), 'How might the brain generate consciousness?', in *From Brains to Con-sciousness*, ed. S. Rose (London: Allen Lane).
Humphrey, N. (1992), *A History of the Mind* (London: Chatto & Windus).
Humphrey, N. (1995), 'The thick moment', in *The Third Culture* ed. J. Brockman (New York: Simon & Schuster).

Humphrey, N. (1999a), 'The privatization of sensation', in *The Evolution of Cognition*, ed. C. Heyes & L. Huber (Cambridge, MA: MIT Press), in press.

Humphrey, N. (1999b), 'Now you see it, now you don't' [commentary on Crick and Koch, 1999], *Neuro-psychoanalysis*, in press.

Kelso, J.A.S. (1995) *Dynamical Patterns: The Self-Organization of Brain and Behavior* (Cambridge, MA: MIT Press)

McGinn, C. (1989), 'Can we solve the mind–body problem?', *Mind*, **98**, pp. 349–66.

McGinn, C. (1993), 'Consciousness and cosmology: hyperdualism ventilated', in *Consciousness*, ed. M. Davies & G.W. Humphreys (Oxford: Blackwell).

Munz, P. (1997), 'The evolution of consciousness — silent neurons and the eloquent mind', *Journal of Social and Evolutionary Systems*, **20**, pp. vii–xxviii.

Newton, I. (1671), 'A letter from Mr. Isaac Newton . . . containing his New Theory about Light and Colours', *Philosophical Transactions of the Royal Society*, **80**, pp. 3075–87.

Penrose, R. (1989), *The Emperor's New Mind* (Oxford: Oxford University Press).

Ramachandran, V.S. & Hirstein, W. (1997), 'Three laws of qualia: what neurology tells us about the biological functions of consciousness', *Journal of Consciousness Studies*, **4** (5–6), pp. 429–57.

Ramsey, A.S. (1954), *Dynamics* (Cambridge: Cambridge University Press).

Reid, T. (1764/1813), *An Inquiry into the Human Mind*, ed. D. Stewart (Charlestown: Samuel Etheridge).

Reid, T. (1785/1813), *Essays on the Intellectual Powers of Man,* ed. D. Stewart (Charlestown: Samuel Etheridge).

Searle, J.R. (1992), *The Rediscovery of the Mind* (Cambridge, MA: MIT Press).

Andy Clark

Phenomenal Immediacy and the Doors of Sensation

Nicholas Humphrey (2000) offers a refreshingly progressive recipe for laying wide the doors of sensation: for understanding the peculiar features of qualitative or sensational experience in terms of the physical or functional facts about brains, bodies and environments. The key move in the treatment is the promotion of a kind of co-ordinated, double-sided tweaking: a careful restatement, with some amendments, of *each* side of the elusive identity statement 'sensational property x = brain state y'. Only after such restatements herd the two kinds of facts into a roughly common arena, Humphrey believes, can some kind of identity story be revealed as coherent, plausible, and explanatorily potent (as an aside, I think everything Nick says is compatible with the claim being pitched at a functional, rather than a brute physical, level, but nothing in the present treatment will hang on whether or not that is so).

To this end, Humphrey first pulls apart the way our sensations inform us about an external world (perception) and the way they proximally feel (sensation), restricting the left hand side of the identity to the latter aspect only. Sensation is then depicted as active rather than passive — as a kind of 'reaching out *to* the body surface with an evaluative response'. The central claim can then be stated: it is that 'what I actually experience as a feeling — the sensation of what is happening to me — is my reading of my own response to it' and reveals not so much something being done to me as 'the way something is being done *by* me' (all the above quotes, page 13). This attractive suggestion — that 'directed self-involvement' lies at the heart of the peculiar or distinctive features of sensation — is then elaborated via a five point parallel between features of feeling a pain in the head and features of performing a hand wave. The parallels serve to increase our sense of the plausibility of an identity claim defined over this tweaked image of sensation and over a comparably tweaked physical or functional story: one that now focuses especially on the five properties themselves (ownership, bodily location, presentness, qualitative modality and phenomenal immediacy). The whole story is then rounded off with some evolutionary conjectures.

I shall not address the evolutionary conjectures here, nor the basic claim about double-sided tweaking (which strikes me as eminently plausible), nor the whole of the five-point parallel. Instead, I shall offer some remarks on just two of the nominated five distinctive features of sensation, and attempt to fill a logical gap in Humphrey's story. The spirit is thus one of (I hope) constructive augmentation.

Journal of Consciousness Studies, **7**, No. 4, 2000, pp. 21–4

The two features I have in mind are numbers four and five on page 14, viz., 'qualitative modality' and 'phenomenal immediacy'. Qualitative modality concerns the way sensation is felt as belonging to a specific modality (visual, olfactory, somatic, etc.). Phenomenal immediacy concerns the way the various features (including the feature of qualitative modality) are in some way 'self-disclosing', i.e. objects of direct and immediate awareness. In each case, Humphrey seeks to better understand the sensational property by analogy with the corresponding property of the simple hand wave (belonging to a class of types of action, and intended — 'authored' — so as to belong to that class: both types of fact that present no special problem in the case of the hand wave).

Concerning phenomenal immediacy, however, it is easy to fear a kind of pernicious circularity in any such story. For there seems to be a clear logical gap between the idea of something's being 'self-disclosing' by being known to 'authored' by the agent herself, and something's being *phenomenally* self-disclosing, i.e. directly known via some distinctive feel or sensation. The mere idea of knowledge of authorship fails to illuminate the question of phenomenal feel, while to assume that the knowledge of authorship comes via the distinctive features of such feels is to introduce qualitative facts on the wrong (right hand) side of the allegedly explanatory equation between sensory phantasms and physical facts. In short, the idea that certain events are self-disclosing insofar as the agent is actively bringing them about leaves open the logical and explanatory gap that Chalmers (1996) and others highlight. Why should knowledge of authorship not be as free of sensational depth and character as, say, knowledge that Paris is the capital of France? Nor is it obvious that the treatment of any of the remaining three features on Humphrey's list does anything to fill this gap. So it looks as if Dennett's 'quicksilver qualia' (Dennett, 1997) have once again fallen through the weave of even our finest-grained physicalist nets.

I want, however, to explore a possible way out of this difficulty. It is a way that strikes me as entirely in the spirit of Humphrey's overall approach, and that differs only in making an extra effort to foreclose the logical and explanatory gap mentioned above. I pursue the story at more length in Clark (2000), but the bare bones look like this.

Imagine a being able to use a visual and an auditory modality to detect a variety of external events, and to be interrogated verbally about it's actions. Now take the case in which the being (agent) detects a colour difference between two visually presented cups.

If we ask the agent about this event (of difference detection) it must surely say one of two things. Either (1) I know nothing about the specific act whereby I detected this difference. I cannot tell you (except perhaps by inference — see below) which modality I used. The answer ('the red cup is on the left') just came to me, *or* (2) I have some kind of direct access to certain aspects of the act of colour-difference detection itself, and thus I know (directly and non-inferentially, at the personal level) that I was using a visual rather than an auditory modality. I am directly aware that I *see* rather than *hear* the difference.

Assuming that (as stipulated) the agent does not merely *infer* the use of the visual modality (for example, by observing that whenever she covers her eyes she cannot make the colour discriminations), and assuming also that the information does not simply come 'tagged' as visual courtesy of an extra unstructured signal meaning (roughly) 'this information gathered by vision', the agent *must* (I argue) claim that there is something distinctive that it is like to acquire the knowledge by visual means. She must say this simply because she has what I (Clark, 2000) gloss as 'direct unmediated access to the act of detection'. Such direct access is not to be conceived as access via awareness of a mysterious sensational quality. Rather, the claim is that the idea that there is a special sensational quality present is forced upon the agent by the fact that she has direct unmediated access to certain distinctive physical or functional features of the visual encoding. Appropriate physical features might be special features of the inner vehicles of visual (rather than, say, auditory) contents (see also Güzeldere, 1997). Appropriate functional vehicles might include, for example, the special way visually gathered information is poised for the control of distinctive kinds of action and intervention (see, for example, Grush, 1998; Evans, 1985). Which kind of empirical story is to be preferred I leave open here. What counts, either way, is that the agent has some kind of direct unmediated access to distinctive nonphenomenal properties of the act of detection itself. Where such access is available, the agent must judge there to be a difference in what it is like to gather information by sight rather than by, for example, hearing. At this point, the worrying gap isolated earlier has ceased to exist. We have entered a necessarily zombie-free zone, a zone where facts about access imply (but do not assume) a difference in how things are sensationally given.

What I am chasing here, it should be clear, is an account of the features that Humphrey dubs 'immediacy' and 'qualitative modality' such that immediate (in my terms 'direct, non-inferential') knowledge of qualitative modality implies (but does not circularly assume) phenomenal or sensational feel. The argument has some of the flavour of both Dennett's (1991) deflationary story and Lycan's (1997) story about perceptual self-monitoring (to pin down the differences, see Clark, 2000). And in line with Humphrey's own strictures, it stresses the role of our access to our own self-authored acts of detection rather than to features of the states of affairs detected.

If this argument, or anything roughly similar, works, then there is a way to tell Humphrey's story that avoids any potential circularity in the notion of 'phenomenal immediacy': a way that shows why, in certain special cases (those involving direct unmediated access to an act of detection) there is (*pace* Block, 1995) no gap between facts about access and facts about qualia or sensations. Such a story does not, of course, explain *all* the facts about qualia. At best it shows why we must judge there to be something it is like to, for example, see differences between colours . But it does not show why the experience (say, of red) should feel exactly *like that*, rather than like something else. Perhaps a fully worked out version of Humphrey's larger evolutionary story can help us here? Or perhaps this residual question is itself ill posed. At the very least, I believe Humphrey's careful and progressive story, once insulated from the threat of circularity, holds out the hope of real progress in an argumentative arena depressingly close to a stalemate.[1]

References

Block, N. (1995), 'On a confusion about a function of consciousness', *Behavioral & Brain Sciences*, **18**, pp. 227–87.

---

[1] Thanks to David Chalmers, Brian McLaughlin, Jesse Prinz, Terry Dartnall and Pete Mandik for valuable discussion of the argument concerning direct unmediated access to acts of detection.

Chalmers, D. (1996), *The Conscious Mind* (New York: Oxford University Press).

Clark, A. (2000), 'A case where access implies qualia?', *Analysis*.

Dennett, D. (1991), *Consciousness Explained* (New York: Little Brown & Co.).

Dennett, D. (1997), 'Quining qualia', in *The Nature of Consciousness*, ed. N. Block, O. Flanagan and G. Güzeldere (Cambridge, MA: MIT Press).

Evans, G. (1985), 'Molyneux's question', in *The Collected Papers of Gareth Evans*, ed. G. Evans (London: Oxford University Press).

Grush, G. (1998), 'Skill and spatial content', *Electronic Journal of Analytic Philosophy*, **6**, (http://www.phil.indiana.edu/ejap/).

Güzeldere, G. (1997), 'Is consciousness the perception of what passes in one's own mind?', in *The Nature of Consciousness*, ed. N. Block, O. Flanagan and G. Güzeldere (Cambridge, MA: MIT Press).

Humphrey, N. (2000), 'How to solve the mind–body problem', *Journal of Consciousness Studies*, **7** (4), pp. 5–20 (this issue).

Lycan, W. (1997), 'Consciousness as internal monitoring', in *The Nature of Consciousness*, ed. N. Block, O. Flanagan and G. Güzeldere (Cambridge, MA: MIT Press).

Daniel Dennett

It's Not a Bug, It's a Feature

Today, the planet has plenty of conscious beings on it; three billion years ago, it had none.[1] What happened in the interim was a lot of evolution, with features emerging gradually, in one order or another. Figuring out what order and why is very likely a good way to reduce perplexity, because one thing we have learned from the voyage of the Beagle and its magnificent wake is that puzzling features of contemporary phenomena often are fossil traces of earlier adaptations. As the great biologist D'Arcy Thompson once said, 'Everything is the way it is because it got that way'. And even when we can't remotely confirm our Just So Stories about how things got the way they are, the exercise can be salutary, since it forces us to ask (and try to answer) questions that might otherwise never occur to us. We do have to get the left and right sides of our equation to match in dimensionality — I am grateful to Humphrey (2000)for this useful proposal about how to think about the issues — and adding wrinkles on the right needs to be motivated by, and in the end justified by, more than the sheer need for a few more dimensions. As Just So Stories go, Humphrey's account of the emergence of sensation is a valuable one, traversing ground that must be traversed one way or another, and providing along the way some reasonable grounds for supposing things happened roughly the way he supposes.

Humphrey has convinced me that *something like* his distinction between visual sensation and visual perception needs to be drawn, but rather than focus on relatively minor problems I have with specifics of his account, I want to articulate and then rebut a blanket 'objection' that I anticipate will be widespread in other commentaries on this essay:

> A robot could meet all of Humphrey's dimensional conditions. Yes, of course, Humphrey frames the design of his conscious organism in terms of evolutionary redesign, and stresses the ecological interplay that helps set the costs and benefits for this exercise in R-and-D, but nothing he proposes in the way of an evolutionary innovation is *in principle* beyond the reach of roboticists. For instance, he says at a midway point in his Just So Story: ' . . . the animal is actively responding to stimulation with public bodily activity, and its experience or proto-experience of sensation (if we can now call it that) arises from its monitoring of its own command signals for these sensory responses'. I presume that a robot can 'actively' respond and is capable of at least '*proto*-experience of

---

[1] You will agree unless you are one of those who wants to grant consciousness to bacteria and other single-celled life forms. Granting a smidgen — or perhaps a 'quantum' — of micro-consciousness to bacteria is a logically available option, with nothing to recommend it and many problems, as I explain elsewhere (Dennett, forthcoming).

Journal of Consciousness Studies, **7**, No. 4, 2000, pp. 25–7

sensation'; if these presumptions are not so, Humphrey is smuggling in something crucial with these terms. So Humphrey is, in spite of his assurances, only dealing with the
easy problems of consciousness, since even if he is right about everything he says, he has
provided an account only of those features of consciousness that are robot-friendly,
functionalistic, a matter of 'complex behavioral dispositions' — and, as he says of
Dennett's earlier attempt, such an account, 'while defensible in his own terms, has
proved too far removed from most people's intuitions to be persuasive. . .'

I think the correct response to this objection is as follows: Yes, indeed, in principle
a robot *could* instantiate Humphrey's theory. But not just *any* robot. It would have to
be a robot quite unlike the typical robots of both reality and imagination, and whether
or not it could *actually* be created is an empirical question. (A conscious robot, like a
splittable atom, may be held to be 'impossible by definition' — but definitions can go
extinct when they've outlived their usefulness.) Humphrey makes an important point
when he claims that our sensory states are descendants of more primitive earlier systems of response-to-stimulation, and as such come already linked quite tightly to
action-propensities that can be suppressed or deflected only by mounting layers of
competing forces and coalitions; additional structures that modify the settings and
import of the ancestral types, while preserving their evaluative valence. So we'd have
to permit the roboticists to give their robot a *virtual* past, with pain-wiggles and
salt-wiggles and the like, leaving their fossil traces on the (hand-coded, not naturally
selected) designs of the 'descendant' systems. It would have to be a robot with a particular sort of organization, the sort of organization that *might* be artificially created
but that would arise naturally by something like the process described in Humphrey's
Just So Story. It would have to be an embodied robot, like Cog (Dennett, 1998, chapter 9).[2] Its nano-machinery would not necessarily have to be protein molecules (like
ours), but it would display both the functions *and dysfunctions* that we display,
thanks to our evolutionary heritage. For instance, it would find some topics harder to
concentrate on than others simply because the sensory baggage that those topics car-
ried was, for 'prehistorical' reasons, harder to overcome. A trivial example: it would-
n't just show human performance deficits on the Stroop test (reading colour names
printed in ink of non-matching colours); it would prefer red ink for some topics and
green ink for others, for reasons it found impossible to articulate. Multiply this case
by a thousand. In every circumstance in which people manifest — and *sometimes*
reflect on — such differential loading (was the element Humphrey calls sensation
present or not, and if present, what was its evaluative valence, if any?) the robot
would do likewise because it, too, was endowed with an organization having the
strengths and concomitant weaknesses provided by such an evolutionary history.

Now the question to consider is whether a robot that matched human function and
dysfunction at such a grain level would be conscious. If you are sure that the answer
is *no*, you should reflect on what your reason could possibly be, given the deliberate
sketchiness of the foregoing description. If your reason is only that you insist on
maintaining a vision of consciousness that is *automatically* proof against any kind of
robot, you are just retroactively adding dimensions — one might suspect: *making up*
dimensions — to put on the left hand side of the equation. In sum, the fact that

---

[2]   And yes, it is only 'practical' considerations that demand this; 'in principle' it could live its whole life
      as a brain in a vat, though the vat would have to be Vast [Dennett, 1995, p. 109] in its complexity in
      order to provide the full force of *virtual* embodiment.

Humphrey's account leaves open the prospect of a conscious robot is in its favour, not a problem. As they say in the software world, 'It's not a bug, it's a feature'.

References

Dennett, D.C. (1995), *Darwin's Dangerous Idea* (New York: Simon & Schuster).
Dennett, D.C. (1998), *Brainchildren* (Cambridge, MA: MIT Press).
Dennett, D.C. (forthcoming), 'The Zombic Hunch: The extinction of an intuition?', *Philosophy*.
Humphrey, N. (2000), 'How to solve the mind–body problem', *Journal of Consciousness Studies*, **7** (4), pp. 5–20 (this issue).

Naomi Eilan

Primitive Consciousness and the 'Hard Problem'

If we think intuitively and non-professionally about the evolution of consciousness, the following is a compelling thought. What the emergence of consciousness made possible, uniquely in the natural world, was the capacity for representing the world, and, hence, for acquiring knowledge about it. This is the kind of thought that surfaces when, for example, we make explicit what lies behind wondering whether a frog, as compared to a dog, say, is conscious. The thought that it might not be is closely bound up with doubts about whether there is a world out there for it. Such doubts are reinforced by neurophysiological and psychological theories to the effect that its purpose-specific, bug-detecting input does not provide for a connected spatial representation of the environment. Or rather there is no need to postulate such a representation in order to explain its tongue lashing out to catch the bug. Reflecting further, it seems that something else critical is lacking, or not necessarily present, in the explanation of the movement of the frog's tongue, namely the kind of appeal we normally make to another major feature we think consciousness introduced into world — wants, emotions, desires, or, more generally, affective states and events. Without their existence, the intuition is, all we have are, at most, non-conscious information processing mechanisms. And when we ask what is required for desires and the like to be in play, we seem to come full circle. For whether or not it is correct to speak of individual desires for specific things in the world seems to have some kind of dependence on whether the organism in question is capable of representing those things, which in turn seems to depend on whether there is a world out there for it. And finally we tend to think that it is only when we have in play this kind of explanation of movement that action and agency appear on the scene.

There is, then, an *a priori* intuitive connection of some kind between our concepts of consciousness, knowledge-yielding representation, action and affect. And let us say that when we have the right kind of connection instantiated, we have the minimum needed for a conscious perspective on the environment, and, hence, a subject of consciousness. If I have understood two of Nick Humphrey's (2000) general intuitions here correctly, one is that we have to get right the exact nature of this basic connection before going on to engage fruitfully with the so-called hard question of consciousness, namely the question of the place of consciousness in nature. Hence the interest in spelling out a story about the evolution of the most primitive form of

Journal of Consciousness Studies, **7**, No. 4, 2000, pp. 28–39

consciousness. His second central intuition is that we must and can do better than rest with claims to the effect that we lack the conceptual wherewithal to give a coherent story about how consciousness fits into the natural world. On both these large issues I am in complete agreement with him. I think we differ, however, in how to make good these intuitions. In what follows, I want to raise some problems I see for his views, if I have understood them, beginning with issues arising from the steps he distinguishes in the evolutionary emergence of consciousness. I then move on to problems with the kind of distinction he draws between perception and sensation. I end with some questions about how he understands the hard question and about what he thinks counts as answering it.

I: The Primitive Form of Consciousness

The steps I want to focus on in the story Humphrey sketches about the emergence of consciousness are the ones in which we have a transition from the capacity to represent oneself and what is happening on the surfaces of one's skin (step one, labelled 'sensation'), to the capacity to represent the external world (step two, labelled 'perception'). In the first step the animal asks itself, according to Humphrey, 'what is happening to me?' (for example, when its surface is stimulated by salt or light). At this stage 'the animal neither knows nor cares *where the stimulation comes from*, let alone what the stimulation may imply about the world *beyond* its body'. It is only later that, as he puts it, 'animals hit upon the idea of using the information contained in surface body stimulation for the novel purpose of asking "what is happening out there?"'. And it is at this stage that we get the transition from sensation to perception. According to Humphrey, the second question requires a quite different kind of information processing from that involved in sensation. Whereas sensational information processing is 'affect-laden, modality-specific and body-centred', and provides information that is 'qualitative, transient and subjective', perception of the external world provides 'a more neutral, abstract, body-independent representation of the outside world' where the information is 'quantitative, analytical, permanent and objective'. (Humphrey, 2000, pp. 16–17).

The obvious question that arises here is what is supposed to be the content of the 'body-centred representation' in primitive sensation? Is the body represented as a physical object, or, less demandingly, as a spatially bounded area? If it is, then the capacity to do so surely requires the capacity to represent the space in which it is located, namely the external world. So the second step is already presupposed in the first. But if the internal representations do not represent the body as a spatially bounded surface, it is not only not clear what it *is* being represented as, but, more importantly, there is nothing in the cognitive repertoire of the creature which it could use to raise the question 'what is going on out there?'.

As far as spatial representation is concerned, then, the body cannot have the kind of priority Humphrey seems to assign to it. One way of responding here might be to concede this point and then to rephrase the central idea here as follows. First, as far as space goes, the representation of space and of the body as in it come together; we do not have one without the other. Second, the representation of the body nonetheless has a kind of explanatory priority by virtue of its role in generating affect-ladeness, without which there is no consciousness in play, but at best mere information processing.

Let us look at each of these claims in turn. The intuitive objection to the first claim is that there are more primitive forms of spatial representation than ones in which the body is represented as one object among others in the spatial environment. The idea here is that the ability to do the latter yields an extremely sophisticated conception of space, one which brings with it both objectivity and self consciousness. The most primitive forms of spatial representation of the environment, in this view, are immersed or engaged precisely in that one does not have this detached view of one-self as one object among others in the space represented. Less metaphorically, consider, for example, Gibson's idea that variations in the perceptual flow contain information about one's own movements, and that the content of such information is in this respect 'self-specific'. (Gibson, 1979; Neisser, 1993). The self-specificity here does not involve the representation of oneself as an object. What it means to say that the information is self-specific is wholly cashed in terms of built-in connections between the content of the perceptions and dispositions of the organism to correct its movements relative to the input.

Now one might think, rightly in my view, that simply having this kind of story in play is not sufficient for having in play the representation of a spatially connected world out there. We only have the minimum needed for the latter, the claim would be, when we have a creature who can re-identify places as the same again over time and possible movement. And the idea might then be that this does require the representing of oneself as one object among others.

But that is not true, or certainly not obviously so. Let us call that which enables such re-identification the 'frame of reference' used. The critical question is whether the frame of reference used is one in which the animal has to be able to place itself, as one among the other objects, in the space represented. There are various ways of spelling out the most primitive frame of reference in which such a capacity is not required. (See Brewer and Pears, 1999; Campbell, 1994, Chapter 1). For example, one might say that we have primitive re-identification of places in play when we have a creature who can update its directional vectors as it moves relative to them (so that places perceived as on the left are perceived, as it moves, as being progressively and systematically first in the front and then to the right and so forth). And such capacities do not require representing oneself as one of the objects in the environment represented. One way of putting this is to say that the contents of primitive representations are monadic rather relational, to borrow a distinction from John Campbell. Places are represented as being on the left and then on the right and so forth, instead of 'on the left of me'. (Campbell, 1994, p. 119).

Now it is, of course, possible to claim that this is not good enough, appealing only to general considerations about spatial representation. But I don't think this is the line Humphrey would choose. Rather, the point of the body for him is that it introduces affect-laden representations. I think Humphrey is exactly right to insist on the importance of such an ingredient if we are to do justice to our intuitive notion of a conscious perspective, to be distinguished from a mere information processor. But this of itself does not give the representation of the body an obvious or essential role. Many affective, consciousness-related states are actually outwardly directed. Fear, attraction (to food or mates etc.) and even hunger can be thought of, in their most primitive form, as infecting perceptions of things in the environment rather than the representation of the body. Given this, one might equally insist that we only have the right kind of spatial representations of the environment in play — that is, the kind needed for having consciousness in play — when they themselves are affect-laden. On this view, the most primitive spatial representations we are looking at are ones in which features of the environment are perceived as good to eat or to hide in, and so forth; that is, as having significance for the animal's well-being (so that the most primitive form of content represents something like affect-laden Gibsonian affordances). On the face of it, then, affect can have the kind of consciousness-conferring role Humphrey assigns it, if I have understood him, whether it is inner or outer directed.

To sum up the first kind of concern about the stepwise story Humphrey tells: the body cannot have an explanatory priority as far as the representation of space is concerned. If we insist that the representation of the body in space is in there from the beginning, the best we could say is that it comes together with the representation of the environment. But, from the perspective of explaining spatial representation only, there are more primitive forms of spatial representation we could appeal to in explaining the beginnings of the representation of a world out there for subjects. The thought we then considered was that we nonetheless have to think of the representation of the body as in there from the start in order to distinguish mere information processing from consciousness, because it is in virtue of the capacity to represent the body that affect gets linked to representation. The claim so far has been that there is no special advantage, from this perspective, in linking affect to the representation of the body rather than of environment. I turn in the next section to considering what I think is a definite disadvantage in so doing.

II: Sensation and Perception
(Or 'Consciousness of' and Phenomenal Consciousness)

A central plank in Humphrey's approach to consciousness is the insistence on the distinction between sensation and perception. When we smell a rose, say,

> two separate and parallel things happen: we both feel the sweet smell at our nostrils and we perceive the external presence of the rose. . . . In general we can and do use the evidence of sensory stimulation to provide a 'subject centred affect-laden representation of what's happening to me', *and* to provide 'an objective, affectively neutral representation of what's happening out there' (Humphrey, 2000, pp. 11–12, quoting Humphrey, 1992).

Perception and sensation, then, often co-occur. This has led many philosophers and psychologists to conflate them. But this is a mistake, says Humphrey. The concepts are distinct in that they refer to two quite distinct properties a mental event may have.

Much of what he says on this score has the ring of various recent 'two-concept' claims made about consciousness. Thus we find general claims that we should distinguish two concepts of mind, the phenomenal and the psychological (David Chalmers, 1996), and more specific ones, for example the claim that we need two concepts of consciousness, phenomenal and access (Ned Block, 1995). To the extent that Humphrey's distinction should be read in this spirit, then it inherits the problems of these other two-concept claims. In this section I focus on problems such approaches have in explaining the notion of perceptual consciousness of the environment. In the next I turn to more general problems for interpreting and making good Humphrey's proposals for solving the mind–body problem.

My procedure in this section will be as follows. I will describe and raise difficulties for the notion of perceptual consciousness of the environment that emerges from Ned Block's distinction between phenomenal and access consciousness (in Block, 1995). I will then suggest that either Humphrey's distinction between sensation and perception has exactly the same difficulties in explaining 'consciousness of', for closely related reasons, or it doesn't have these problems, but that then he must abandon the way the distinction is used by him to motivate a two-step evolutionary story.

Blindsighted subjects are subjects who, following damage to their visual cortext, become 'functionally blind' in particluar areas of their visual field — that is, they fail to respond spontaneously, in action or judgement, to stimulation from those areas. But as several neuropsychologists have shown, when induced to guess what is in the functionally blind area they can do so for quite a wide range of properties, while simultaneuously denying that they have any visual experience. The reason blindsight is appealed to in discussions of consciousness is that it serves as a useful tool for examining the relation between distinct ingredients in our intuitive concept of consciousness. In particular, it is said to show the possibility of the following combination of states of affairs.

(1) The subject has perceptual information about the environment (inferred from his capacity to guess some of the properties in the 'functionally blind' area of the visual field, and, when induced, to direct appropriate movements towards them).
(2) There is no consciousness of the portion of the environment about which the information is taken to exist (there is no 'transitive consciousness').
(3) The perception is not in the stream of consciousness; not 'in mind' (there is no 'intransitive consciousness').
(4) There is no phenomenal consciousness; no experience.
(5) The perceptions do not provide the basis for rational judgements and rationally guided action.

Block is interested in the relation between 4 and 5. He labels the consciousness referred in to in 4 'phenomenal' and the way in which perceptions stand poised for rational control of beliefs and actions 'access conscious'. He wants to argue that although these usually come together, they are, in fact, distinct properties a perception (or any mental state) may have. I want to raise one problem for this claim, which, in turn, raises immediate difficulties for the kind of distinction I think Humphrey wants to draw between sensation and perception.

In order to show that we can have, in the perceptual case, access consciousness without phenomenal consciousness, Block has us imagine a 'superblindsighter'. Suppose a blindsighter could be trained to guess at will what is in the functionally blind areas of his visual field; that is, without being prompted to do so. In such a case, says Block, visual information will simply 'pop into mind' in the way solutions to problems do. The superblindsighter contrasts these kinds of cases with his normal perceptual experiences, in which there is something it is like, a phenomenal feel. The perceptual information, in such a case, will be accessible without having any phenomenal properties.

The most immediate and obvious puzzle this claim raises is the following. As Block himself describes it, the judgement about the world, based on the superly blindsighted events, strikes the subject as coming out of the blue. That is, it does not appear to him to be rationally justified. The perceptual input does not provide him with evidence for his judgement. So we do not have here the kind of access Block himself says is connected with our concept of consciousness. Now, if we ask what is lacking here, one thought is that were the perception in mind — intransitively conscious — then such a justification would be forthcoming. So, in the occurrent, perceptual case, we need a notion of access which is such that if a state is accessible, it follows that it is in mind. Suppose then we ask: what is needed for the latter? The intuitive answer is that when perceptions yield consciousness of the world — awareness of it — this suffices both for 'in-mindedness', and for rational access. And if we ask now: why do not the superblindsighter's perceptions or the blindsighter's yield awareness of the environment? What do we need in order for there to be in play not merely information about the environment, but awareness of it? And here we reach intuitively for the lacking phenomenal consciousness. In some way, when phenomenal consciousness is in play then we have consciousness of the world, a presence of the world to the subject, rather than mere information about it.

So in the normal case — intransitive consciousness, 'consciousness of' — phenomenology and justifying access come together. Let us say that when they do, perceptions *present* the world to the subject as being such and such. It is this presentation of the world to the subject, or its appearance as such and such to the subject, which (a) gives the perception its evidential status, (b) secures its being in the stream of consciousness and (c) at the same time yields something it is like for the subject, from her perspective. It is presence of the world to the subject, thus understood, that is lacking in both blindsight and superblindsight.

How is presence to be explained? In particular, what account should we give of the relation between the content of the experience, which provides the content for the judgement it justifies on the one hand, and the phenomenal properties of the experience on the other? There are basically two options. One is to introduce non-representational phenomenal properties, which yield something it is like from the subject's perspective and then to say that the *de facto* co-occurrence of non-phenomenal representational properties with non-representational phenomena yields the kind of presence we are after. The other is to say the relevant phenomenal properties are a special kind of representational property. As Block makes clear, the first is his preferred option. Indeed, this is the option one must adopt if one is to say that the relation between phenomenal and access consciousness is at most causal. Let us see, then, whether the option Block opts for could do the work of explaining presence.

Recall, a central constraint is that the notion of presence we come up with is that its possession by a perception brings with it, in addition to phenomenology, (a) evidential status and (b) location in the stream of consciousness. Suppose phenomenology is explained exhaustively by appeal to non-representational properties. Then, with respect to (a), there are two routes one might take in explaining how the addition of such properties to representational status secures evidential status. Either by means of giving rise to the judgement: such and such sensations are in the normal course of events accompanied or caused by a perceptual state with such and such representational properties, so I must have perceptions with such contents and they are my reason for judging that such and such is the case in the world. Or, more directly: such and such sensations are normally caused by such and such a state of the world and that is my reason for judging such and such to be the case. But it is familiarly dubious whether such indirect reflective judgements could actually provide an alternative justification. And even when we bracket sceptical doubts, our own perceptions, we think, give rise to direct non-reflective justifications for our judgements. As to (b), location in the stream of consciousness, neither of these reflective routes makes the perceptual representation *accessible* to the subject in a way which guarantees in-mindedness. Intuitively, the subject could issue such judgements while the representational properties of the perceptual state remain wholly non-conscious; outside her stream of consciousness.

So the requisite notion of presence cannot be got right if we assume that the phenomenal aspect of normal experiences is to be explained by appeal to non-representational properties. The alternative is to say that what we need is an account of how representational and phenomenal aspects of experience are interwoven with each other in such a way as to yield such presence of the world to the subject, and to treat this as a *sui generis* kind of representational property a perception can have. But to say this is to reject both the independence of access and phenomenal consciousness and the independence of consciousness of and phenomenal consciousness.

Turning now to Humphrey, the question for his distinction between perception and sensation is this. Either the way he draws the distinction commits him to a distinction of the kind I have been criticizing between representational and phenomenal properties, or it does not. If it does commit him to it then it looks as if he cannot get right the notion of 'consciousness of', and the way it is to be distinguished from merely having information about the environment. But if it does not commit him to it then, on the face of it, we lose both the motivation for, and the substance of, the two-step story he tells. Another way of putting the point is this. In the previous section I suggested that the representation of the body as spatial cannot be independent of and prior to the representation of the space in which it is located. Spatially, the body can play no primary role. There I suggested that the point of the body was really to introduce affect, but that affect could go into perceptions of the environment as well, so on this score, too, the representation of the body need have no priority. The point of this section has been that if we are to get right the notion of consciousness of the environment, as opposed to the mere possession of information about it, then the notion of perception that we need is not, *contra* Humphrey, conceptually independent of the properties he assigns sensation. And, once this is conceded, we lose any motivation for insisting that the representation of the body has a primary role to play in the emergence of consciousness.

III: Consciousness and Nature

Suppose you have a visual experience, as of a rabbit in front of you, and are aware of this experience and think of it as an experience, with such and such phenomenal properties. Let us call the way of thinking made available to you in virtue of undergoing the experience 'introspection'; the predicates you employ when introspecting these properties 'phenomenal' (P) predicates; and the modes of presentation they express 'P' modes of presentation. Suppose at the same time someone is probing your brain and watching various neurones firing away in response to the external stimulation. And let us suppose the person watching your neurones is armed with predicates used in something we may call the 'brain sciences' which covers everything from physiology to computational information processing theories. I will call these 'scientific' (S) predicates, and the modes of presentation they express 'S' modes of presentation.

On a common version of the prevailing account of The Hard Problem, the central question we should be asking is: could P and S predicates ever be referring to the same properties? Let us call this the Identity Question version of the Hard Problem. The central problematic it confronts is stated by Thomas Nagel in 'What it is like to be a bat?' as follows.

> Usually, when we are told that X is Y we know how it is supposed to be true, but that depends on a conceptual or theoretical background and is not conveyed by the 'is' alone. We know how both 'X' and 'Y' refer, and the kinds of things to which they refer, and we have a rough idea how the referential paths might converge on a single thing, be it an object, a person, a process, an event, or whatever. But when the two terms of identification are very disparate it may not be so clear how it could be true. We may not have even a rough idea of how the referential paths converge or what kinds of things they might converge on, and a theoretical framework may have to be supplied to enable us to understand this. Without the framework, an air of mysticism surrounds the identification (Nagel, 1979, pp. 176–7).

Nagel then goes on to argue that precisely such a framework is lacking when we are told that conscious states are identical to brain states, and that properties of conscious states are identical to some brain properties.

The first thought here is that if any pair of S and P predicates do refer to the same property, they will be doing so in different ways, expressing different modes of presentation of the property, for any such identity claim is informative. The second thought is that normally, when we say that two modes of presentation have the same referent, we have some story about 'how the referential paths converge'. Thus we have a theory about why 2+2 and 4 refer to the same number; a story about why the Morning Star and Evening Star are different modes of presentation of the same planet, and so forth. The third thought then is, in its most minimal form, that we do not have any such story in the case of P and S predicates. And because there is no such story or 'theory', an air of mysticism surrounds the identification.

So, to recapitulate on this reading.

(1) The basic question we should be asking is: Do S and P predicates ever refer to the same properties, or, more generally, home in on the same realm of reference? (The Identity Question)

(2) The basic challenge we encounter is that, on the face of it, we do not know how to start answering the question because we have no theory of how the referential paths converge. (The Radical Disparateness thesis)

Humphrey, if I have understood him, agrees that the way to address the place of consciousness nature is to ask the Identity Question. And, if I have understood him, he thinks that we can deliver a positive answer and that the route to doing so is in showing that the radical disparateness we *prima facie* encounter is actually illusory. And he thinks that the evolutionary story he tells shows how to dispel the feeling of disparateness. It is with respect to these claims that I am least sure if I have followed the argument. So let me lay out how I understand both the disparateness claim and what is required for denying it, and then go on to raise some questions for Humphrey.

There are various ways of formulating the disparateness claim, and so various ways of denying it, but the disparateness claim that seems closest to Humphrey's concerns would go something like this. Two modes of presentation are disparate in the requisite sense, on this account, when there is no overlap between the substantive concepts each one draws on in individuating the property it refers to. So, for example, there is no overlap in the substantive concepts used to individuate colours and numbers. And Nagel's formulation of the 'problem of consciousness' can be put, in these terms, as follows. In the brain/consciousness case we seem to have the kind of disparateness we have in the number/colour case. One way of developing this idea is to be found in David Chalmers' claim to the effect that we have two wholly independent concepts of mind.

> The first is the phenomenal concept of mind. This is the concept of mind as conscious experience, and of a mental state as a consciously experienced state. This is the most perplexing aspect of mind . . . . The second is the psychological concept of mind. This is the concept of mind as the causal or explanatory basis of behaviour. According to the psychological concept, it matters little whether a mental state is conscious or not. What matters is the role it plays in cognitive economy. On the phenomenal concept, mind is characterized by the way it feels; on the psychological concept, mind is characterized by what it does. There should be no question of competition between the two notions of mind. Neither of them is the correct analysis. They cover different phenomena, both of which are quite real (Chalmers, 1996, p. 11).

As I will be reading it, to adopt a two-concept account in support of the radical disparateness claim is to say that we can give an exhaustive account of the causal/physical ingredients in our everyday psychological concepts without any essential reference to phenomenal ingredients. And we can give an exhaustive account of the phenomenal ingredients without any reference to the causal physical ingredients. There is no substantive overlap. Consider now the property of being visual (as opposed to tactual or auditory) that one might apply to one's experiences when introspecting and describing what they are like. Applying the two-concept approach, the claim would be that when we make introspectively-based judgements about the properties of our experiences, in particular about the sensory type of experience one is undergoing, the concepts we use are actually ambiguous. One's judgement to the effect one is seeing a white rabbit, say, should actually be analysed as consisting of two claims. One is about the instantiation of properties identified introspectively by the use of purely phenomenal concepts; the second is a claim about the instantiation of purely psychologically identified properties. Each of these can be individuated without any reference to the materials used, essentially, in individuating the other. The consequence of this is that any further scientific casual discoveries or theories about the workings of the brain will go over into an elaboration of our psychological concept only and will have no impact on, or internal connection with, our phenomenal concept.

Chalmers himself is a dualist. He thinks that when we say we are having a visual experience, say, each concept refers to a different property, where these properties are normally co-instantiated. But it is important to note that the two-concept view, as so far outlined, is shared by very many statements of the problem of consciousness, in which the position finally advocated is physicalist or mysterian. On these, the radically disparate concepts are merely ways of thinking of what may be a single underlying reality. So, on these accounts, visualness may be a single property — but what makes the problem of consciousness so hard is that we have two mutually independent ways of thinking about this property and because of this we *prima facie* do not know how to begin to make sense of their having a common referent.

Now, the most radical denial that our mental concepts are disparate in this way would involve endorsing what I will call the 'one-concept' view. On this view the lesson we should draw from the operation of our everyday concepts of perception is that our mental concepts are such that the phenomenology and spatial/causal explanatory ingredients are interdependent. The kind of causal ingredients relevant here, in the case of perception, are those we find in what is often referred to as our 'primitive theory of perception', where grasping such a theory (and hence the concept of perception) involves understanding what the conditions of perceivability in the various modalities come to (that one must be in the right place, at the right time, that there must be nothing in the way and so forth). The one-concept claim says that we cannot get the phenomenology right, individuate the phenomenological ingredient in our everyday concepts, without essential appeal to this kind of spatial/casual explanatory framework; and we cannot get the explanatory framework right without essential appeal to the phenomenology. The implication of this is that there are certain *a priori* restrictions on the level and kind of discoveries about the brain that could be used in explaining, say, what vision is.

Where does Humphrey stand here? *Some* of what he says suggests a general intention to argue for a one-concept view, for example when he speaks of closing the gap from both the phenomenological and the scientific ends simultaneously. And this aim, to the extent he has it, is in my view well worth having and trying to push forward. The reason for engaging in the question of the place of consciousness in nature in the first place is that we are, on the face of it, what one might call 'common sense realists' about consciousness. We think that what goes on in the world affects how things are with us, phenomenologically speaking, and that how things are with us affects physical events in the world. The major trouble with the two-concept theory is that if it were true then there would not be even *prima facie* internal justification for treating our phenomenal states and their properties as the causes and effects of how things are in the spatio/casual world. For on the two-concept theory, any reference to causal mechanisms is taken over by the 'psychological', functional concept — the phenomenal concepts we use have no causal implications at all. On this view it should be a wild unwarranted leap in the dark, at best, to link phenomenology to causal happenings in the world. Generalizing, either our ordinary thinking about consciousness does commit us to realism about phenomenal properties, or it does not. If the two- concept story is right, then our ordinary thinking does not commit us to any such realism and there is nothing to be baffled about; no question about the place of consciousness in nature. If, on the other hand, we are committed to realism, then the two-concept story is wrong, and should be abandoned when we set out to give an account of what realism about phenomenal properties comes to.

However, abandoning the two-concept approach is very much easier said than done. To so much as take the one-concept account seriously as an option requires a radical overhaul of a great number of well-entrenched philosophical intuitions and presuppositions — perhaps more radical than Humphrey wants, certainly more than he delivers in this paper. It is true that some of what he actually does say suggests commitment to the view that, in the case of somatic sensations at least, we cannot get phenomenology right without appeal to physical objects, actions, causation and the like. This, if I have understood it, lies behind the idea that sensation is, essentially, a modification of a way of directing actions towards one's body — subtract the body and the action and you are left with nothing. But, as we noted, he doesn't extend this claim to perception. Indeed, some of what he says about the relation between sensation and perception sounds very close to the kind of two-concept claim Chalmers makes about perception, except that the phenomenal properties are referred to as sensational.

More importantly, however, he does nothing to argue for the other side of the one-concept claim, the idea that the individuation of the causally relevant psychological properties of minds must bring in how things are for the subject, from her perspective. And it is here, surely, that we begin to engage with the really hard bit of the hard problem. As an example of something that has to be taken on here, consider Chalmers' two-concept claim about perception. 'It can be taken wholly psychologically, denoting the process whereby cognitive systems are sensitive to the environmental stimuli in such a way that the resulting states play a certain role in directing cognitive processes. . . . But it can also be taken phenomenally, involving the conscious experience of what is perceived.' So long as this kind of phenomenology-free individuation of the causal component in our mental concepts is allowed to be correct, we have done nothing to engage with the central intuition that drives people into adopting dualism, eliminativism, reduction and mysterianism, all of which, if I have understood him, Humphrey wants to avoid. This is the claim that we can get a complete description of the causal workings of our minds without any (non-reductive) appeal to what things are like for the subject, from her perspective. Phenomenal consciousness is, in brief, causally epiphenomenal. If the one-concept story involves a new move here, we need to understand how it locks causation into phenomenology.

One central idea that needs to be engaged with here is this. Causation is part of the objective world. On a prevalent account of objectivity, objective representations are representations of the world from no point of view. They can be understood and used by anyone, irrespective of their actual situation in the world, their experiences and so forth. In contrast, one of the most robust intuitions about knowing what an experience is like is that this can only be done from the inside, meaning in a way that depends essentially on one's capacity to have experiences of the kind one is describing. So, on the above conception of objectivity, the problem is that getting the causal story right is, in part, a matter of eschewing precisely the kind of experience-dependent concepts we think are required for knowing what an experience is like from the inside. Any convincing one-concept interdependence approach here will have to make good the claim that the use of experience-dependent ways of thinking to individuate the casual ingredient in our mental concepts does not *a priori* rule out the kind of objectivity that is required for getting causation into the picture in the first place. So long as the equation of objective representations with representations from no point of view is retained, this remains an impossible task, and the one-concept approach is not even in the running. In fact, for what it is worth, I think this notion of objectivity should anyway be challenged on independent grounds. Chief among these is the problem that it cannot explain the way in which spatial thought provides for the idea of an objective world, because such thought relies essentially on demonstratives to fix reference to particular objects. Whatever line one takes here, however, the general point is that short of dealing with this side of the one-concept response to the radical disparateness challenge, it is not clear how the conscious-mind/body problem is being seriously engaged with.

Finally: the Identity Question Humphrey says he is setting out to answer actually dissolves away, we lose it as the 'hard question' of consciousness, if we do adopt the one-concept approach. For if neither the phenomenal nor the spatio-causal ingredients in our concepts of perception can be got right without essential appeal to the other, then we lose the two concepts in terms of which the identity question is formulated. Of course this does not lose us hard questions about how to reconcile scientific views of the brain and phenomenal concepts, but they get relocated into questions not of identity, but of mechanisms, in a way that is familiar from discussions of mental causation. The question becomes: how do scientific discoveries slot into the kind of primitive theories of perception we have? But this is no longer a mind–body problem, for our primitive theories of perception appeal essentially to spatial and causal ingredients. Humphrey, however, places himself squarely in a tradition that does treat the Identity Question as the hard question of consciousness, so in this respect too he cannot be adopting the one-concept approach. But if he isn't then I just don't see how the radical disparateness claim is being undermined; undermined, that is, without appeal to strong reductive or eliminativist claims about phenomenal consciousness, neither of which, as noted above, Humphrey (rightly in my view) wants to adopt.

References

Block, Ned (1995), 'On a confusion about a function of consciousness', *Brain and Behavioral Sciences*, **18**, pp. 227–87.

Brewer, Bill and Pears, Julian (1999), 'Frames of reference', in *Spatial Representation: Problems in Philosophy and Psychology*, ed. N. Eilan, R. McCarthy and B. Brewer (Oxford: Oxford University Press).

Campbell, John (1994), *Past, Space and Self* (Cambridge, MA: MIT Press).

Chalmers, David (1996), *The Conscious Mind* (Oxford: Oxford University Press).

Gibson, J.J. (1979), *The Ecological Approach to Visual Perception* (Boston: Houghton Mifflin).

Humphrey, N. (1992), *A History of the Mind*, (London: Chatto & Windus).

Humphrey, N. (2000), 'How to solve the mind–body problem', *Journal of Consciousness Studies*, **7** (4), pp. 5–20 (this issue).

Nagel, Thomas (1979), 'What is it like to be a bat?', in *Mortal Questions* (New York: Cambridge University Press).

Neisser, Ulric (1993), 'The self perceived', in *The Perceived Self: Ecological and Interpersonal Sources of Self Knowledge*, ed. U. Neisser (Cambridge: Cambridge University Press).

Ralph Ellis

Efferent Brain Processes and the Enactive Approach to Consciousness

Nicholas Humphrey (1992; 2000) argues persuasively that consciousness results from active and efferent rather than passive and afferent functions. These arguments contribute to the mounting recent evidence that consciousness is inseparable from the motivated action planning of creatures that in some sense are organismic and agent-like rather than passively mechanical and reactive in the way that digital computers are. Newton (1996) calls this new approach the 'action theory of understanding'; Varela *et al.* (1993) dubbed it the 'enactive' view of consciousness. It was endorsed in passing by the early Dennett (1969), although he never followed up on it in his later work. According to Dennett, 'No afferent can be said to have a significance "A" until it is "taken" to have the significance "A" by the efferent side of the brain' (Dennett, 1969, p. 74). Luria also stressed the neurophysiology of efferent processes as correlated with consciousness (Luria, 1973, pp. 82–8). Further elaborations of the enactive approach are defended by Ellis (1986; 1990; 1995; 1999a,b; forthcoming), Newton (1982; 1993; 1996), Ellis and Newton (1998), Watt (1998), Thelen and Smith (1994), Jarvilehto (1999) and Gendlin (forthcoming). According to this view, conscious information processing can arise only as the self-regulated action of a self-organizing process that confronts the world as a system of action affordances. While information can be passively absorbed in the form of afferent input, only efferent nervous activity in the interest of a living organism's homeostatic (yet suitably extropic) balance can create consciousness of any information, whether perceptual, imagistic, emotional or intellectual.

If, as Husserl says, we never argue more vigorously than against the ideas we most recently espoused, then perhaps some similar caveat should apply to ideas we still do embrace. As a fellow enactivist myself, I have probably been confronted at various times with most of the objections that can be brought against this theory, some of which it might be helpful to mention here. None of these objections undermines the enactive view. But I believe some of them do legitimately entail caution with regard to the enactive theory's sufficiency to 'solve' the mind–body problem. My view is that the enactive approach is a necessary but not sufficient element in the solution of the mind–body problem.

It is true that any hope of solving the mind–body problem will necessitate taking an enactive approach, because every non-enactive theory inevitably shipwrecks on the

Journal of Consciousness Studies, **7**, No. 4, 2000, pp. 40–50

reefs of this enigma. As Humphrey points out, simply to assert that the mind and body are identical does not enable us to understand how two such incommensurable terms even in principle could be equivalent. Jackson's knowledge argument (1986) well dramatizes this point. If knowing everything that can be known about Jackson's brain does not enable Mary to know what it feels like for Jackson to be obsessively in love with her, then Jackson's brain should not be literally the same as the consciousness it subserves. If two things are identical, then whatever is true for one should be true for the other; knowing all about the one should enable one to know all about the other.

Superficially, the enactive approach appears to avoid the mind–body quagmire quite easily, because by identifying consciousness with an agent-initiated action, we can describe it in ways that make sense both phenomenologically and physically. The action of an organism can be understood in empirical-scientific terms, as the result of a physical system — a self-organizing system, of which biological organisms are examples. And it can also be understood in terms of something that we can experience phenomenologically; everyone knows what it is like to engage in an action. Moreover, the fact that knowing about others' physiology, by itself, cannot tell us how they feel ceases to be such a paradox, since the enactive approach posits that having a feeling is the same as executing an action, and it is obvious that we cannot execute someone else's actions (Ellis and Newton, 1998; Ellis, 1999b).

But serious questions must be addressed to make this move work. First, what is the difference between 'action' and 'mere reaction'? Does a thermostat act, or only 'react'? What if it is an extremely complex thermostat, with a number of feedback mechanisms in it? And if 'action' means the unified, goal-directed action of a motivated and living being, then questions arise about the meaning of these terms. What is the defining difference between living beings and non-living ones? What does it mean to be motivated, rather than cleverly programmed to mechanically pursue an end, as robots do? A thermostat, one might argue, is not motivated in the relevant sense, although it does systematically pursue an end.

If the response here has to do with 'purposefully' as opposed to 'non-purposefully' pursuing an end, then we are involved in a distinction with which twentieth-century science did not do well. There are non-conscious purposeful activities in nature, as when salmon find their way upstream to return to their spawning areas in order to reproduce their species, or when overpopulated lemmings jump into the sea to avoid overshooting the population niche of their species. Presumably, the salmon and lemmings have no conscious awareness that these are the purposes of their activities, but they are purposeful nonetheless. The problem, then, is that purposeful activity cannot simply be defined in terms of conscious end-directed activity; otherwise, to explain consciousness with reference to its end-directed nature would become circular. But the twentieth century has been able to understand purposefulness only as a kind of process that lends itself to anthropomorphism because of its resemblances to the processes that conscious beings can subjectively experience or imagine. On this view, the behaviour of lemmings or salmon is not really purposeful, but only resembles purposeful behaviour. Really, it is just as reactive and causally bottom-up as is the tendency of a thermostat to maintain a temperature. But if a thermostat is not purposeful or living, then certainly building more and more complex thermostats is not going to make them purposeful or living — that was the bitter lesson learned by computationalists who thought that building a more and more complex information processing machine would eventually facilitate building a conscious robot, the crowning feat that artificial intelligence engineers had promised to deliver by the end of the twentieth century. But the more general problem, with which we must all grapple, is understanding what it means for something to be purposeful.

The question of the distinction between enaction and reaction is all the more important because Humphrey — rightly, in my view — nails the entire difference between conscious and non-conscious information processing squarely onto this concept. The most obvious objections from those not familiar with this argument can be satisfied easily enough. Some will object that anticipatory expectations and organismic motivations seem unnecessary for certain types of conscious experiences. While driving a car, we may pay conscious attention to an advertisement on a billboard even though the product advertised has no interest for us. The consciousness seems completely passive, and the notion that it somehow was produced by active and goal-oriented organismic activity rather than from passive and aimless causal inputs seems far-fetched to many people. Is the notion that consciousness always results from agency rather than from passive stimulation really plausible?

This objection overlooks the broad, general organismic interest in the environment; if it is always possible that something in the environment might be important, we must pay a certain amount of attention to objects in the environment in order to discover whether they are important for our purposes. A general curiosity can motivate the active direction of attention to objects that are only possibly important for the organism's purposes. This broad vigilance toward objects in general may not determine attention as precisely as when something happens for which we are already specifically on the lookout, for example, when something suddenly runs across the road in front of us. But increasingly evidence is mounting that, without motivational interest, at least of a general sort, there is no consciousness (see Ellis and Newton, forthcoming). Even when we are disinterestedly 'vegging' in front of the television, no matter how much it may seem that we have no motivational anticipations for what is going to appear next on the screen, this complex network of anticipations will become immediately obvious if the television set should suddenly explode, or turn into a pigeon and fly away. Our feeling of surprise shows that we did have certain expectations about what was going to occur next, very much in the way we do when tracking the movement of a soccer ball. Our looking for the ball is a necessary condition for seeing it, and this looking is motivated by our desire to see it. If the ball turns up where we are not looking, we must reorient our pattern of looking before we can pick it up again.

Another related objection is that attention and conscious awareness are not the same thing. There are studies in which subjects non-consciously learn to execute tasks requiring attention, in the sense that an item must be distinguished from surrounding items and thus becomes a focus point for sensory and cognitive processing, while the surrounding items are not focussed on in this way (Cohen *et al.*, 1990; Bullemer and Nissen, 1990). All of this occurs without any conscious awareness of the item on which 'attention' has been focussed in this way.

The easiest answer to this objection is that, although there can be attention without consciousness, there can be no consciousness without attention. The recent Mack and Rock (1998) perceptual studies clearly bear this out. Subjects who were occupied with an attentional task did not consciously see an irrelevant object, even though it was presented at or near the point of visual fixation, and even though it was presented in such a way that under normal conditions (i.e., in control trials) it would have been seen. So, even though we may not be aware that the directing of attention is taking place during every conscious state — just as we may not be aware that we are focussing our eyes, performing searching movements, etc. — it is necessary nonetheless. We are accustomed to noticing the object of our consciousness rather than the subjective events that make it possible.

I: The Afferent/Efferent Distinction

A more serious kind of problem is posed by the need to distinguish efferent from afferent processes. Humphrey posits that conscious processes must be efferent rather than afferent, since efferent processes are in some sense more active, whereas afferent ones are reactive. Afferent and efferent impulses are easy enough to distinguish in the parts of the nervous system that are outside of the brain, the former conveying information toward the brain, the latter away from it. But once we get inside the brain, it is difficult to say what is afferent and what is efferent.

There is of course a trivial sense in which an impulse, say from the motor cortex to the parietal lobe, is both efferent with respect to the motor cortex (i.e., away from it) and afferent with respect to the parietal lobe (toward it). But in the sense Humphrey is referring to, 'efferent' needs to mean something more significant, and neurophysiologists do sometimes use the term in this more significant sense: 'efferent' can mean 'directed by the central organism, toward the periphery,' as opposed to 'received from the periphery' — and in this sense we could say that an impulse that moves from the motor cortex to the parietal lobe is efferent, since the motor cortex is the prime example of a brain area whose purpose is to command bodily action. Can we meaningfully make this kind of distinction with all brain impulses?

Neurophysiological research shows that the posterior portion of the brain receives incoming input from the senses (Hubel and Wiesel, 1958; Posner and Petersen, 1990; Warrington, 1985). So we might designate these activities as afferent. And it is known that signals from the brain stem and other emotional subcortical areas move upward into the anterior cingulate and prefrontal cortex (Posner and Rothbart, 1992; Gray, 1990; Luria, 1980; Olds, 1977), and from there to less 'central' areas of the brain (if we take the emotional area as 'central'). So signals from the brain stem and prefrontal cortex (as well as those from the brain stem to the prefrontal cortex) might reasonably be regarded as 'efferent' in the needed sense.

But as for the part of the brain 'between' the prefrontal cortex and the posterior areas, more research must be done. There are, of course, differences between what happens in the primary projection areas of the various sensory modalities and the secondary sensory areas and association areas of the parietal and temporal lobes (Aurell, 1984; 1989; Luria, 1973; Sperry, 1966). EEG studies, PET scans, etc. show that incoming sensory signals first activate the primary sensory area which is at the surface of the cortex, and then activate the secondary sensory area (Luria, 1973; Hubel and Wiesel, 1959). This secondary layer adjacent to the primary projection area contains feature detectors that react only to specific features of environmental images — some cells reacting to right angles, some to vertical lines, some to horizontal, etc. So all of that is afferent in the sense Humphrey is interested in.

Consciousness of an object does not occur at the point when only these afferent activities of primary and secondary projection areas of the relevant sensory modality are observed (Aurell, 1989; Posner and Rothbart, 1992). Consciousness occurs only with the efferent activation of the anterior cingulate, prefrontal and parietal areas, and this activation is not a direct causal result of primary or secondary projection area stimulation. That means that, consistently with Humphrey's hypothesis, consciousness does not result passively from causal stimulation. The nerve impulse from the sensory organs (eyes, ears, etc.) to the primary projection area first passes through the thalamus, which, in connection with emotional processes of the upper brain stem, alerts the anterior cingulate and frontal brain areas that some important input might be in the offing. If there is a feeling that there may be something worth paying attention to (an emotional value judgment in relation to the entire organism's homeostatic balance), then the prefrontal cortex begins formulating questions about what kind of information might be coming in from the environment (Luria, 1973; Ellis, 1995), and whether it is likely to be relevant or important. If so, this prompts efferent input to the parietal and secondary sensory areas, resulting somehow in the production of sensory and sensorimotor images. When these imaging activities of efferent areas find synchronized patterns of activity in the afferent areas, such as the primary projection area, only then does perceptual consciousness occur. Without the afferent input, the efferent activity would be experienced as the mental image of a non-present object.

Agent-directed efferent activity as it gives rise to consciousness is well illustrated by the way the frontal lobe, when emotionally motivated, leads to imagistic and cognitive consciousness that also activates other brain areas. Luria sees the frontal lobe as 'formulating the problem' to be solved by the brain (1973, p. 188). Thus, in Luria's view, the frontal lobe, which is clearly efferent, is active when we pose a problem or question to ourselves that requires that we do some thinking. Posner and Rothbart (1992) attribute an analogous role to the anterior cingulate (which is clearly efferent) in directing attention — a function that Mack and Rock (1998) find is essential for conscious perception. The Mack and Rock perceptual experiments show that we are unconscious of objects to which we are completely inattentive. The general rule is borne out: efferent activity is essential to consciousness.

Function rather than structure defines the difference between efferent and afferent in all the examples just discussed. There is no sharp boundary between a completely efferent area and a completely afferent area. The brain uses functional 'modules' (Gazzaniga, 1986) — widely distributed overlapping systems. While efferent activity may be more pronounced in anterior areas, and afferent activity more posterior, this is only because the posterior region receives input from the senses, while the anterior is controlled by the emotional–motivational system, which must determine the direction of attention.

Consciousness always involves efferent activity, defined as neural activity generated by the organism itself, for purposes of its own survival and well-being, rather than from passive stimulation by incoming sensory signals. That is the important point. Consciousness results from a motivated searching operation; efferent activity must select certain incoming data as worthy of attention. Only after executing this purposeful process can the organism focus attention and produce the 'looking-for' consciousness needed for attention and imagery-formation. We know that this imaginal consciousness is associated with parietal activation, driven by frontal and anterior cingulate efferent activity, which in turn is driven by emotional–motivational purposes; this then leads to perceptual consciousness corresponding to the object whose input is activating the primary projection area. The secondary sensory area is the endpoint of a series of efferent activities.

Thus Newton (1993; 1996) shows that perceptual consciousness, by contrast to passive, computer-like processing, always involves imagining what would happen if we were to do something actively (rotate the object, squeeze it, drop it, etc.). If the subjunctive imagination of a possible sensorimotor activity is presupposed even by the perceptual consciousness of an object, then imagination is the most basic building block of perceptual consciousness, and the efferent always has primacy over the afferent. We are conscious of objects according to their action affordances, which can be imagined. This imagining of action affordances is facilitated by the motorically- initiated efferent brain commands that Damasio (1999) calls the 'as if body loop'.

This primacy of the efferent in all consciousness is also consistent with Tucker's (1981) thesis that efferent activity is oriented toward activating motoric behaviour, and that consciousness is largely a truncated, imaginary motoric behaviour. For example, we may remember a piece of music by imagining ourselves playing it. PET scans by Petersen et al. (1990) show that the anterior cingulate and the supplementary motor area — obviously efferent — are even involved in attention to language. And Damasio (1999), in a neurological tradition dating all the way back to Olds (1977), finds that there can be no consciousness unless the basal ganglia interact in certain specific patterns with the cortex. Imagination thus can be viewed as truncated motor behaviour. To imagine an object is 'as if' to anticipate acting in relation to its affordances. Motor neurons, in fact, mature earliest in ontogenesis (Restak, 1984, pp. 46–7). Moreover, Kimura and Archibald (1974), Studdert-Kennedy and Shankweiler (1970), and Liberman et al. (1967) show that speech evolves neurophysiologically as a truncated form of motoric behaviour. To think a word is to imagine ourselves saying the word.

All of this is beautifully illustrated by the Held and Hein (1958) studies in which motoric (obviously efferent) action underlies development of perception in kittens. In essence, the kittens who from earliest infancy had been pulled around in carts by older cats behaved as if they were blind, bumping into objects and falling over edges. Objects 'are seen . . . by means of the visual guidance of action' (Varela et al., 1993, pp. 174–5).

II: Agency and Self-organization

Now if the efferent/afferent distinction is drawn functionally rather than structurally — if 'efferent' means initiated by aim-oriented organismic activity — then the efferent/afferent distinction, in the sense relevant to this discussion, is derivative from the active/passive distinction. And that returns us to our original question: what is the difference between the living, agent-like, active, and purposeful on the one hand, and the non-living, passive, merely reactive or mechanical on the other?

What is needed to make these distinctions work is a notion of self-organization that is well enough articulated in terms of causal processes to ground such distinctions. A thermostat is non-living and non-purposeful, not because it is not composed of carbon and hydrogen, and not because everything it does has a physical cause which is ultimately traceable to its external environment (for, if the data of science are to be believed, that must be true of all of us!); the thermostat is not living or purposeful because of the way thermostats and living things are organized. Self-organizing systems must have a special kind of causal structure, so that we can say 'this process is active — is a purposeful agent — whereas that one is not'.

But the causal power of living organisms is a very difficult question. In a sense, living processes must be just as rigidly and mechanically caused as anything else in the universe. So the notion of the causal power of a living being — the power that makes it 'unified' in such a way that it acts for its own purposes, rather than reacting to external forces — is a logically delicate one.

Self-organization theory seems necessary in addressing this question, and the best-developed current expression of that seems to be 'dynamical systems theory'. Self-organization theory has a rich but recently neglected tradition tracing back through Kauffman (1993) and Monod (1971) to Merleau-Ponty (1942) and the developmental biologists of the early twentieth century who were interested in the way embryos manage to appropriate available physical components to settle into the self-directed pattern of unfolding development (Bertalanffy, 1933/1962).

A self-organizing process can be defined as one whose organization creates a strong tendency to maintain itself across various alternative causal mechanisms at the level of the components making up the system. The structural pattern is not just multiply realizable, but actually plays an active role in appropriating the combinations of substrates needed to maintain the overall pattern. For purposes of applying the theory to the problem of mental causation, and thus to the mind–body problem (for example, Thelen and Smith, 1994; MacCormack and Stamenov, 1996; Freeman, 1975; 1987; Edelman, 1989), the problem is to understand how the system is self-maintaining across multiply realizable substrates, some available subset of which the system actively seeks out, appropriates, replaces, and reproduces.

All biological organisms are self-maintaining in this sense. There is no assumption here that 'artificial' systems could not also manifest such structures. The issue is not whether the system is composed of certain specific elements such as silicon or carbon, but rather the structural dynamics of the system.

Dynamical systems theorists currently elaborate these concepts in terms of open thermodynamic systems, of which biological organisms are examples. Open thermodynamic systems continuously exchange constituent components and energy with their environment, yet maintain homeostatic constancies across these exchanges. These constancies preserve the continuity of the structural organization. A behaviour pattern into which the system has a strong tendency to settle is called an 'attractor' or 'basin of attraction'. The organism learns and remembers new perceptual patterns by creating new basins of attraction structurally related to the learned stimulus pattern (Freeman, 1987; Alexander and Globus, 1996). It remembers a familiar action pattern that the particular stimulus pattern affords; a particularly surprising pattern throws the system into momentary chaos, until holistic reorganization is achieved.

An implication of dynamical systems theory as applied to emotions is that a specific motivation, say the desire to raise my hand, results ultimately from the organism's self-organizing tendency. This self-organizing structure is therefore present, and embodies a tendency for me to want to raise the hand, even before the desire becomes pronounced enough to be a conscious awareness. Thus the 'expectancy wave' accompanying the decision to raise the hand is measurable before I am aware of a decision or desire to raise it (Libet *et al.*, 1983; Young, 1988, pp. 164–6). Expectancy waves (also manifested in Libet's 'readiness potential') indicate that motivational feelings arise out of the organism's generally self-organizing nature.

The upper brain stem (which includes midbrain, PAG, and Raphe nuclei) monitors this chemical homeostasis throughout the entire self-organizing system of the body, and sends efferent commands (via Ach, DA, EN, NE and 5HT) for action aimed at restoring homeostasis. These commands are sent to the thalamus, hypothalamus, cingulate, amygdala, etc. and ultimately through the anterior cingulate and frontal lobes to the rest of the cortex. Efferent (anticipatory) imagery at this point has to do with anticipated actions, which automatically correlate with anticipated object affordances. Afferent feedback from real objects can convert the efferent imagery into perceptual consciousness, but the efferent imagery is already conscious with or without afference. The various deficiencies that can occur in this entire process are illustrated by the different forms of automatism, akinetic mutism, and persistent vegetative states (in which there is minimal consciousness and attention) discussed by Damasio (1999).

III: The Mind–Body Problem

Does such a theory 'solve' the mind–body problem? My view is more modest than Humphrey's. First of all, it is important to be clear about what the mind–body problem consists of, and to acknowledge its true difficulty. We should distinguish between the mind–body problem on the one hand, and on the other hand the 'hard problem of consciousness' that Chalmers talks about. All too often in recent consciousness research, these two problems are conflated.

The mind–body problem is not just a question that is difficult to answer, but a paradox. On the one hand, consciousness does not seem to be equivalent with its physiological substratum, for reasons of the kind the knowledge argument presents; but on the other hand, if consciousness were not equivalent with something physical, then we would be confronted with the well-known problems of dualism, which are formidable.

Let's not forget what the main problem of dualism is. It is that it fails to make sense of the causal power of consciousness. When I raise my hand, certain physical nervous events are completely sufficient to account for the hand's going up. Yet it feels to me as if my conscious decision to raise it is necessary to make it go up. If the physical antecedents were sufficient to make it go up, then nothing else should be necessary to make it go up. So we want to say that the physical antecedents are sufficient for the hand's going up, and at the same time that something else, a conscious decision, is necessary for it. This seems like a logical contradiction, unless we assume that the physical and mental events are equivalent. Of course, if two events are equivalent, then they both can be both necessary and sufficient for the same outcome. That was the main argument that prompted cognitive theorists to embrace psychophysical identity theories in the first place — because they eliminate the problem of mental causation. But by avoiding the Charybdis of mental causation in this way, strict identity theories are consumed by the Scylla of the knowledge argument. The mind–body problem, then, is essentially a logical paradox resulting from the causal role of consciousness.

The fact that mind and body seem indescribable in commensurable languages — which leads to Chalmers' 'hard problem' — is really a much easier problem than the mind–body problem. The hard problem merely shows that we have a phenomenon, consciousness, that in principle is difficult to explain. If we give a physical explanation for a state of consciousness, X, by showing what caused its physical substrata, Y, to occur, the question will always remain as to why the physical event Y has the property of consciousness.

However, this 'hard problem' is not as serious a problem as the mind–body problem. The mind–body problem does not consist merely in the fact that consciousness is difficult to explain, but rather in the apparent fact that every possible explanation for it will still lead to self-contradictions, because no proposed explanation can explain how a mental event can cause a physical one without thereby rendering the physical antecedents of the event insufficient to cause it. While the hard problem points out the difficulty in understanding why some physical events have consciousness, the mind–body problem points out that the very notion of there being both physical and conscious events is self-contradictory, because as soon as we posit this apparent fact, there seems to be no way to resolve its contradictory causal implications.

To solve the mind–body problem will therefore require more than just to show how the same event can be described in a way that makes both physical and phenomenological sense. It requires also that we show how the causal properties of the physical and phenomenological events do not contradict each other.

Now suppose that, as Humphrey has argued, consciousness can occur only as a result of an organismic activity, and is equivalent with efferent rather than with afferent nervous activity. The question remains as to what kind of causal power this consciousness-equated-with-efferent-activity has. Does it resolve Jackson's knowledge argument? Suppose a biologist knows all about self-organizing thermodynamic systems, and all about efferent nervous activity. Will that enable the biologist to know what the subject's consciousness is like? This does not seem obviously to follow. It seems entirely conceivable that the biologist could observe Jackson's nervous system, in full knowledge of the fact that it is only the efferent activity that is conscious, and still not know what Jackson's consciousness — for example, his being in love with Mary — feels like.

Monod's and Kauffman's concepts of self-organization do not entail a dualism or a causal interactionism: the process does not cause the behaviour of its substratum elements. Instead, the behaviour of each substratum element is caused by other substratum level components that are both necessary and sufficient, under the given background conditions, to bring about that behaviour. But the self-organization of the organism in which this behaviour occurs is partly responsible for having set up, at each moment, the given background conditions under which those antecedents are necessary and sufficient for those consequences. If the antecedents needed for a behaviour are not available, the self-organizing organism is structured so that it can change some of its other functions to allow some other mechanism, for example a 'shunt mechanism', to be used as the necessary and sufficient antecedent of that same behaviour. A typical example is the reorganization of brain function in mild stroke recovery. Even though the specific behaviour of each substratum element is caused by a substratum level component which is necessary and sufficient to produce it under the given background conditions, the structure of the self-organizing process as a whole is such that those given circumstances will tend to be changed when that is what is needed to maintain the overall process as such.

The complex self-organizing process constitutive of the emotionally motivated efferent processes needed for the subject's phenomenal consciousness are experientially accessible only from the standpoint of the organism that executes them, because conscious experiencing *per se* entails executing rather than merely observing emotional processes. That is why self-organization is the key to solving the mind–body problem — because it promises to address the paradox of mental causation without requiring an out and out rejection of either horn of the dilemma: causal closure on the one hand, and the fact of mental causation on the other.

The enactive approach points us in the direction we must go if we are to solve the mind–body problem, but it only provides a necessary, not a sufficient set of conditions needed for this solution. What must be explained is how a self-organizing or dynamical system can have a causal power over its own substrata, which is not reducible to the sum of the actions of the substrata, while at the same time causal closure is not violated at the substratum level. That is a difficult problem in its own right, and will require more sophisticated causal analyses than have yet been accomplished (for further discussion, see Ellis, 1995, 1999a, 1999b, forthcoming). However, any such causal analyses must use a theory of self-organization as their starting point, since only a dynamical system promises to offer the possibility of a system's having the power to appropriate substratum elements into its own basins of attraction, rather than letting those basins be merely a higher-level description of the independent actions of the substrata. That is why I believe that an enactive theory is necessary for any solution to the mind–body problem.

References

Alexander, David and Globus, Gordon (1996), 'Edge of chaos dynamics in recursively organized neural systems', in *Fractals of Brain, Fractals of Mind*, ed. Earl MacCormac and Maxim Stamenov (Amsterdam: John Benjamins).

Aurell, Carl G. (1984), 'Perception: A model comprising two modes of consciousness. Addendum II: Emotion incorporated', *Perceptual and Motor Skills*, **58**, pp. 180–2.

Aurell, Carl G. (1989), 'Man's triune conscious mind', *Perceptual and Motor Skills*, **68**, pp. 747–54.

Bertalanffy, Ludwig von (1933/1962), *Modern Theories of Development* (New York: Harper).

Bullemer, P. and Nissen, M.J. (1990), 'Attentional orienting in the expression of procedural knowledge', paper presented at meeting of the Psychonomic Society, New Orleans, April 1990.

Chalmers, David (1995), 'Facing up to the problem of consciousness', *Journal of Consciousness Studies*, **2** (3), pp. 200–19.

Cohen, Asher; Ivry, Richard and Keele, Steven (1990), 'Attention and structure in sequence learning', *Journal of Experimental Psychology: Learning, Memory and Cognition*, **16**, pp. 17–30.

Damasio, Antonio (1999), *The Feeling of What Happens* (New York: Harcourt Brace).

Dennett, Daniel (1969), *Content and Consciousness* (London: Routledge & Kegan Paul).

Edelman, Gerald (1989), *The Remembered Present* (New York: Basic Books).

Ellis, Ralph D. (1986), *An Ontology of Consciousness* (Dordrecht: Kluwer/Martinus Nijhoff).

Ellis, Ralph D. (1990), 'Afferent–efferent connections and "neutrality-modifications" in imaginative and perceptual consciousness', *Man and World*, **23**, pp. 23–33.

Ellis, Ralph D. (1995), *Questioning Consciousness: The Interplay of Imagery, Cognition and Emotion in the Human Brain* (Amsterdam: John Benjamins).

Ellis, Ralph D. (1999a), 'Integrating neuroscience and phenomenology in the study of consciousness', *Journal of Phenomenological Psychology*, **30**, pp. 18–47.

Ellis, Ralph D. (1999b), 'Why isn't consciousness empirically observable?' Forthcoming in *Journal of Mind and Behavior*.

Ellis, Ralph D. (forthcoming), 'Consciousness, self-organization, and the process–substratum relation: Rethinking non-reductive physicalism', *Philosophical Psychology*.

Ellis, Ralph D. and Newton, Natika (1998), 'Three paradoxes of phenomenal consciousness: Bridging the explanatory gap', *Journal of Consciousness Studies*, **5** (4), pp. 419–42.

Ellis, Ralph D. and Newton, Natika (ed. forthcoming), *The Caldron of Consciousness: Affect, Motivation, and Self-Organization* (Amsterdam: John Benjamins).

Freeman, Walter (1975), *Mass Action in the Nervous System* (New York: Academic Press).

Freeman, Walter (1987), 'Simulation of chaotic EEG patterns with a dynamic model of the olfactory system', *Biological Cybernetics*, **56**, pp. 139–50.

Gazzaniga, Michael (1986), *Mind Matters* (Cambridge, MA: MIT Press).

Gendlin, Eugene (forthcoming), 'The "mind"/"body" problem', in Ellis and Newton (forthcoming).

Gray, Jeffrey (1990), 'Brain systems that mediate both emotion and cognition', *Cognition and Emotion*, **4**, pp. 269–88.

Held, Richard and Hein, Alan (1958), 'Adaptation of disarranged hand–eye coordination contingent upon re-afferent stimulation', *Perceptual and Motor Skills*, **8**, pp. 87–90.

Hubel, David H. and Wiesel, Torsten N. (1959), 'Receptive fields of single neurons in the cat's striate cortex', *Journal of Physiology*, **148**, pp. 574–91.

Humphrey, Nicholas (1992), *A History of the Mind* (London: Chatto & Windus).

Humphrey, N. (2000), 'How to solve the mind–body problem', *Journal of Consciousness Studies*, **7** (4), pp. 5–20 (this issue).

Jackson, Frank (1986). 'What Mary didn't know', *Journal of Philosophy*, **83**, pp. 291–5.

Jarvilehto, Timo (1999), 'Efference knowledge', *Psycoloquy*, **9**, www.cogsci.soton.ac.uk/psyc-bin/newpsy?article=9.83&submit=View+Article.

Kauffman, Stuart (1993), *The Origins of Order* (Oxford: Oxford University Press).

Kimura, Doreen, and Archibald, Y. (1974), 'Motor functions of the left hemisphere', *Brain*, **97**, pp. 337–50.

Liberman, A.M., Cooper, F.S., Shankweiler, D. and Studdert-Kennedy, M. (1967), 'Perceptions of the speech code', *Psychological Review*, **74**, pp. 431–61.

Libet, Benjamin; Curtis, A.G.; Wright, E.W. and Pearl, D.K. (1983), 'Time of conscious intention to act in relation to onset of cerebral activity (readiness-potential). The unconscious initiation of a freely voluntary act', *Brain*, **106**, p. 640.

Luria, Alexander R. (1973), *The Working Brain* (New York: Basic Books).

Luria, Alexander R. (1980), *Higher Cortical Functions in Man*, 2nd ed. (New York: Basic Books).

MacCormack, Earl and Stamenov, Maxim (ed. 1996), *Fractals of Brain, Fractals of Mind* (Amsterdam: John Benjamins).

Mack, Arien and Rock, Irvin (1998), *Inattentional Blindness* (Cambridge, MA: MIT/Bradford).

Merleau-Ponty, Maurice (1942), *The Structure of Behavior* (Boston, MA: Beacon, 1963).

Monod, Jacques (1971), *Chance and Necessity* (New York: Random House).

Newton, Natika (1982), 'Experience and imagery', *Southern Journal of Philosophy*, **20**, pp. 475–87.

Newton, Natika (1993), 'The sensorimotor theory of cognition', *Pragmatics & Cognition*, **1**, pp. 267–305.

Newton, Natika (1996), *Foundations of Understanding* (Amsterdam: John Benjamins).

Olds, James (1977), *Drives and Reinforcement: Behavioral Studies of Hypothalamic Functions* (New York: Raven).

Petersen, S.E., Fox, P.T., Snyder, A.Z. and Raichle, M.E. (1990), 'Activation of extrastriate and frontal cortical areas by visual words and word-like stimuli', *Science*, **249**, pp. 1041–4.

Posner, Michael I. and Petersen, S.E. (1990), 'The attention system of the human brain', *Annual Review of Neuroscience*, **13**, pp. 25–42.

Posner, Michael I. and Rothbart, Mary K. (1992), 'Attentional mechanisms and conscious experience', in *The Neuropsychology of Consciousness*, ed. A.D. Milner and M.D. Rugg (London: Academic Press).

Restak, Richard (1984), *The Brain* (New York: Bantam).

Sperry, R.W. (1966), The great cerebral commissure', in *Frontiers of Psychological Research*, ed. Stanley Coopersmith (San Francisco, CA: W.H. Freeman).

Studdert-Kennedy, M. and Shankweiler, D. (1970), 'Hemispheric specialization for speech perception', *Journal of the Acoustical Society of America*, **48**, pp. 579–94.

Thelen, Esther and Smith, Linda (1994), *A Dynamic Systems Approach to the Development of Cognition and Action* (Cambridge, MA: MIT/ Bradford).

Tucker, Don (1981), 'Lateral brain function, emotion and conceptualization', *Psychological Bulletin*, **89**, pp. 19–43.

Varela, Francisco; Thompson, Evan and Rosch, Eleanor (1993), *The Embodied Mind* (Cambridge, MA: MIT Press).

Warrington, E.K. (1985), 'Visual deficits associated with occipital lobe lesions in man', *Pontificiae Academiae Scientiarum Scripta Varia*, **54**, pp. 247–61.

Watt, Douglas (1998), 'Affect and the "hard problem": Neurodevelopmental and corticolimbic network issues', *Consciousness Research Abstracts: Toward a Science of Consciousness*, Tucson 1998, pp. 91–92.

Young, John Z. (1988), *Philosophy and the Brain* (Oxford: Oxford University Press).

Valerie Gray Hardcastle

Hard Things Made Hard

Nicholas Humphrey (2000) is interested in illustrating how it is that the mind is the brain. We can think of him as taking up David Chalmers' and Joe Levine's challenge to solve the so-called hard problem, to bridge the so-called explanatory gap. For after being convinced, as we surely are, that minds are housed in brains via the activity of neurons, we still need to *explain* why that should be the case. Why is it that our lumpy grey matter should contain consciousness? Even if we agree that it does, we still need to arrange the facts so that having minded brains is a patently obvious truth.

Humphrey has the insight that the ways we describe both our mental states and our brain states are probably wrong and this prevents us from seeing why it is that minds are brains. We need to correct both sides of the identity equation. So far, so good.

The difficulty is that his corrections don't work, on either side. Let us first consider what he says about our conscious mental states. He considers them to be sensations, as distinct from perceptions. Our conscious states are self-centred experiences of bodily stimulation, feelings about 'what's happening *now* to *me* and how *I* feel about it' (p. 12). These contrast with other, related, mental states: judgments about what the external world is like out there. Conscious experiences are active creations. We 'reach out *to* the body surface with an evaluative response' (p. 13). Consciousness isn't played out before a homunculi audience on a Cartesian theatre; instead, we are both the playwrights and the actors. Better: we are improvisation artists.

Let us leave to one side the question of who or what it is that is supposed to be doing the reaching, reacting, creating and assume that we will be able to cash out these metaphors at some point later. I want to examine whether it makes good neurobiological sense to say that pain just is 'reaching out to the body surface in a painy way' (p. 15). I believe it does not. As a consequence, I think that explaining away the explanatory gap is still a hard thing to do.

Of course, we cannot literally reach out to our bodily surface to experience our periphery's reaction to some noxious stimulus since our efferent reach stops at the dorsal horn in our pain processing system (cf. Hardcastle, 1999). At best, pain is going to be our reaction to our spinal column's reaction to our transducers. But maybe this revision is okay. What counts for a conscious experience, we are told, is our internal response to our bodily response. So presumably nociceptive information comes up our neural fibres through the dorsal horn and thalamus and into our cortex. Once there, pain information almost literally lights up the entire brain. Motor, somato- sensory, cingulate, and frontal cortices all respond to noxious stimuli. (Other

Journal of Consciousness Studies, **7**, No. 4, 2000, pp. 51–3

areas do too, but these seem to be the main regions of interest, at least according to the somewhat dubious subtraction method in imaging studies.) Which part is our reaction to our reaction — the conscious sensation — and which is merely the reaction itself?

One might think that the motor response would be the reaction to our initial pain reaction, but Humphrey tells us that this is not so. Conscious experience is detached from our behavioural responses. So motor response is something else entirely. This leaves us with either somatosensory, cingulate, or frontal cortex as the place where consciousness occurs. But how, I ask, can we determine which area is processing information already there (the reaction to the reaction) as opposed to information on its way up (the reaction itself)? For that matter, how can we distinguish the conscious sensation of a sharp grinding pain in our foot from our perception that tissue damage is occurring to our toes?

One natural way to get a handle on this question would be to perform the obvious lesion studies and simply cut out different areas of cortex to see whether we still feel pain (or feel painly), or we merely perceive pain, or we just have pain without perception or sensation. Unfortunately, the experiments we and Mother Nature have so unkindly performed on humans don't generate clear answers (one reason why the hard problem is hard, though not hard in the way Chalmers thinks). Frontal lobotomies do not seem to diminish the sensation of pain exactly, but they do make us no longer care that we are in pain. (Is this perceiving pain without the sensation? Maybe, except the mental state of feeling-but-not-caring-about-it-anymore is clearly conscious.) Removing parts of somatosensory or cingulate cortex can sometimes remove our sensations of pain. When it does so, it also removes any perception of pain. But in this case, it is no longer clear that we have pain at all in any interesting sense, never mind whether we are perceiving or sensing our pain reactions. There isn't anything we are reacting *to* anymore.

So we are stuck. At least, *I* am stuck. I agree that I do not simply passively react to incoming stimuli. What I sense, perceive, think, and feel are things my brain constructs using previous experience and current inputs. But even granting that this is true, I don't see how knowing this fact helps me connect my occurrent conscious states with concomitant brain activity. Indeed, knowing this fact only makes consciousness more complicated because it blurs the distinctions that Humphrey so neatly draws between sensation, perception, and our bodily reactions. All those things happen at more or less the same time in more or less the same place in my head. (For a quick demonstration of my bald assertion, try to separate visual sensation from visual perception. We don't 'feel redly' about parts of our visual field; at least, we don't do so consciously. Consciously, we can't help but see red as red objects located out there in the world. We project our visual sensations as something external to us. Is this projected sensation now not a sensation at all, but a perception? If so, then what happened to the sensation?)

What about Humphrey's revisions of the brain side of the mind/brain equation? Here I have less to say. Humphrey claims to be giving us a way to match the 'dimensions' of the mind with the 'dimensions' of the brain. What he actually gives us, though, is a just-so story about how it is that creatures could have evolved sensations via natural selection. But that, I take it, isn't particularly mysterious. There is a clear selective advantage to organisms that can react to their environment, a greater advantage to those who can react proactively, and an even greater advantage to those who can remember what has happened before and rehearse what they might do the next time around. For me to see with clarity that the units in which I describe the conscious mind are identical to the units I describe some part of the brain, I will need something other than tales from evolutionary history. I need a way to distinguish, from the brain's point of view, conscious experience from the rest.

But here is where the hard problem gets really hard. Cortex is cortex, as many have remarked. Nothing particularly interesting differentiates visual cortex from auditory cortex from frontal cortex from somatosensory cortex. We don't have any markers for consciousness. At the level of neurons, networks, and areas, consciousness seems to disappear.

Some philosophers lose hope at this point; others develop unusual metaphysics to help them cope with the dearth of data. I myself maintain a stubborn faith in science that we will all get this sorted out one day, without having to confess to innate stupidity and without having to admit new fundamental substances into the universe. But these reactions are fairly inconsequential in the face of Humphrey's problem, which is figuring out how it might make sense to explain the conscious mind in terms of brain activity. I agree with Humphrey that we have done a laughable job in defining what we mean by consciousness. And Humphrey makes a serious stab at getting out important characteristics of conscious experience. Unfortunately, what he says does not square with known brain physiology. He is on the right track, I believe. It is just that the hard problem is harder than he originally envisioned.

References

Hardcastle, V.G. (1999), *The Myth of Pain* (Cambridge, MA: MIT Press).
Humphrey, N. (2000), 'How to solve the mind–body problem', *Journal of Consciousness Studies*, **7** (4), pp. 5–20 (this issue).

Stevan Harnad

Correlation vs. Causality

How/Why the Mind–Body Problem is Hard

[B]rain-imaging studies . . . demonstrate in ever more detail how specific kinds of mental activity (as reported by a mindful subject) are precisely correlated with specific patterns of brain activity (as recorded by external instruments). (Humphrey, 2000, p. 6.)

Mind/Brain (M/B) correlations: We've known about them (dimly) for decades, probably centuries. And that's still all we've got with brain imaging; and that's all we'll have even when we get the correspondence fine-tuned right down to the last mental 'just noticeable difference' and its corresponding molecule.

But the Mind/Body Problem (M/BP) is about *causation*, not correlation. And its solution (if there is one) will require a mechanism in which the mental component somehow manages to play a causal role of its own, rather than just supervening superfluously on other, non-mental components that look for all the world as if they can do the full causal job perfectly well without it (thank you very much). Correlations confirm that M does indeed 'supervene' on B, but causality is needed to show how/why M is not supererogatory; and that's the hard part.

Nick Humphrey's heroic attempt is informative — and some of it might even be correct, functionally speaking — but alas, it, too, fails to furnish the missing causal link for the mental component, which continues to dangle in his account, non-functionally. Hence the only problems Humphrey solves are the 'easy' ones, not the M/BP.

[S]uppose, by analogy, that . . . 'atmospheric-imaging' experiments [demonstrate] that whenever there is a visible shaft of lightning in the air there is a corresponding electrical discharge. We might soon be confident that the lightning and the electrical discharge are aspects of one and the same thing. (p. 6)

Such analogies are (famously) inapplicable to the M/BP (Nagel, 1974; 1986): There is no problem about seeing two sets of empirical observations as 'aspects' of the same thing, given a causal model that unifies them. But there is no such causal model in the case of the M/BP. For, unlike all other empirical observations, such as lightning/electricity (or water/H_2O, heat/molecular-motion, life/biogenetic-function, matter/energy, etc.), in the special case of M/B, the correlated phenomena are not of the same *kind*. And that's precisely what makes this particular set of 'correlations' different — and problematic. So the forecast that M/B will simply turn out to be yet another set of correlations like the rest is unpromising.

Journal of Consciousness Studies, **7**, No. 4, 2000, pp. 54–61

Empirically detectable shafts of lightning and empirically detectable electrical discharges are the same kind of thing (empirical data, detectable by instruments). So are empirically detectable brain activities and empirically detectable behaviour and circumstances. So when I say or act out that something hurts (especially when something is indeed damaging my tissues), and the accompanying brain-image is neural activity in my nociceptor system, we do have a correlation between things of the same kind, exactly as in the case of the lightning. And out of that correlation we can construct a causal theory of nociceptive function (tissue injury, avoidance, learning, recall, etc.).

But when the correlate in question is my *feeling* of pain, we're in another ballpark: there's now an explanatory gap that neither the nociceptive theory (which is only a functional theory of tissue-damage-related *doing*) nor any amount of reconfirmation of the tightness of the correlation can close.

So maybe what Humphrey means to highlight in the lightning case is not the correlation between the two sets of empirical data, but between the empirical data and an underlying causal factor that explains the data. That's fine too, but then the analogy with M/B correlations in imaging is irrelevant, and we are talking about a causal explanation: and if so, what *is* that underlying causal factor in the case of the M/BP? All I see is unexplicated correlations. (Note that the neural functions and the behavioural functions and their interrelations do get explicated, but their *mental* correlations do not.)

Nor is it a matter of 'deducing one from the other *a priori*' (even physics doesn't do that, only mathematics does). The 'laws' of physics are not necessary but contingent; so are their boundary conditions. So this is a red herring. The real problem is about causal explanation in the special case of M/B. Consciousness seems fated to be a causal dangler no matter how tight the coupling and how minute the predictability. It's like perfect weather forecasting without the underlying meteorological theory.

(Remember: neural and behavioural functions are not at issue; mental ones are. The correlations of a purely behavioural neuroscience would not be problematic in any way; it's the causal status of the *mental* component that is at the root of the M/BP. The causality in M/B theory is invariably 'third-party' causality: the underlying neural mechanism causes both the brain/body's functional neural/behavioural states *and* the fact that they happen to be mental states. The trick is to show — *functionally*, if that's the route one elects to take — how/why the mentality is *not* functionally superfluous; just reaffirming that it's causally hard-wired somehow to its functional substrate is not an answer.)

> [W]ith lightning, [t]he physico-chemical causes that underlie the identity [were] discovered through further experimental research and new theorizing. Now the question is whether the same strategy will work for mind and brain. (p. 6.)

It is indeed, and the question arises because of the obvious *dis*analogies: public ('third person') data, as in *all* the other analogies, vs. private ('first person') data. There's a start. And then there's the disanalogy about the (independent) causal role of the private-stuff ('qualia' = feelings): it had better not try to exert any, on pain of telekinetic dualism. Which leaves the usual question of why it's dangling there, then, epiphenomenally. A 'functionalist' would have expected a better answer, a *functional* one. But it's whenever we try to face squarely the question of what causal role feelings could possibly have that we draw a blank (unless we cheat by 'identifying' feelings with something *else* — such as a neural correlate, thereby begging the question!).

Humphrey wishes to distance his own position from two non-starters, those of Chalmers (1996) and McGinn (1989):

> Chalmers [1996] . . . argues [that] consciousness just happens to be a fundamental, non-derivative, property of matter. (p. 6.)

One must agree with Humphrey that such dicta are unedifying. Here is a one-line summary of Chalmers' message: 'The M/BP is *hard*!' So what? How does that help? It's a good pull-up, for those who have simplistic quick fixes, but other than that it is tautological: it wouldn't be the long-standing problem it is if it weren't 'hard'. The question is: is it soluble at all?

> McGinn [1989] believes that . . . certain kinds of understanding . . . must forever lie beyond our intellectual reach [for example, the M/BP]. (p. 7.)

Little substance in that position either, in my opinion. I too happen to think the M/BP's insoluble, but not because of any limitation of the human mind. Indeed, I don't know what is even meant by saying that there may indeed exist a 'solution' to the M/BP, but not one that the mind can ever know! There is nothing here that is analogous in any way to the (epistemic?) constraints underlying Gödel unprovability, quantum indeterminacy, statistical–mechanical indeterminacy, unproven mathematical conjectures, halting problems, the many-body problem, the limits of measurement, the limits of memory, the limits of technology, the limits of computation, NP-completeness, the limits of time, the limits of 'language' (no idea what the last might even mean), etc. Those are all red herrings and false analogies.

Nor is it clear why in his own approach Humphrey wants to obscure the M/BP with formalism ('dimensions', 'equations', 'identities'). The problem is clear, hard, and staring us informally in the face: I have feelings. Undoubtedly the feelings are in some way caused by and identical to ('supervene on') brain process/structures, but it is not at all clear *how*, and even less clear *why*. That's the M/BP. No 'equation' to write down; no 'terms'. And the 'incommensurability' is the name of the game (or of the problem)!

Inputs and outputs can be connected, functionally, computationally. But feelings are another story (a hard one!). If we 'characterize' feelings computationally or functionally, we have simply begged the question, and changed the subject — to a discussion of the relation between brain function and computational (or other) function.

> Most of the states of interest to psychologists . . . remembering, perceiving, wanting, talking, thinking, and so on are . . . amenable to . . . functional analysis. (p. 8.)

In every respect except the *relevant* one, which is that they are *qualitative*, feeling states. They will be amenable to *informational* analysis, and to *behavioural* and *neural* analysis, but their feelingness will remain a dangler — and that's the point! That's what makes the M/BP the problem it is. The functional stuff would all go through fine — behaviourally, computationally — *if* we were all just feelingless zombies. But we're not. And that's the problem (Harnad, 1995; 2001).

> [R]ecalling that today is Tuesday = activity of neurons in the calendula nucleus. . . . But [these] are notoriously the 'easy' cases. . . . No one it seems has the least idea how to characterize the phenomenal experience of redness in functional terms. (pp. 8–9.)

This is too quick. There is *nothing special* about 'detecting red,' compared to 're-calling that X' or 'inferring that Y'. These can *all* be treated functionally (i.e., as transpiring in a zombie), in precisely the same way. There are I/O conditions under which certain psychophysical capabilities in the 'chromoceptive task' domain are adaptive for our species, hence our brains have evolved the functional mechanisms for processing objects with reflective surfaces, etc. But why/how does doing and being able to do that kind of thing *feel like* something? Back to square one, and it's exactly the *same* square for both the 'cognitive/intentional' cases Humphrey thinks are easier (recalling X), and the more patently phenomenal/qualitative ones that wear their hardness more on their sleeves (detecting red).

In reality, *every* mental capacity has both an easy and a hard *aspect*: the functional aspect is easy, the feeling aspect is hard. But it's the feeling aspect that makes it mental! So there's only one M/BP, and that's the hard one. The rest is just mindless zombie functionalism (a branch of reverse bioengineering that is not particularly 'easier' empirically than any other area of science).

Now we arrive at what will be the core insight, which Humphrey attributes to Reid:

> [S]ensory awareness is an activity. We do not have pains, we get to be pained. This is an extraordinarily sophisticated insight [of Reid's]. (p. 13.)

In my opinion Reid provides no insight here. The M/BP has always abutted onto various forms of scepticism — scepticism about the external world, scepticism about other minds. The problem of 'hallucination' (an apparent external object of experience, when in reality there is no external object) has sometimes been folded into the M/BP. From this follows this eagerness to distinguish external object-based experiences like feeling tree-barks from completely internal ones, like feeling moods (I leave out the awkward intermediate case of feeling headaches).

No illumination follows from adopting these distinctions. *Yes*, some of the sceptical problems (not induction, but definitely solipsism and other-minds) are lemmas of the M/BP. But the M/BP is primary. Solve that and those bits of idealism will be trivial by comparison (and will probably vanish).

But don't try to subordinate the (unsolved) theorem to the derivative lemma! Never mind the distinction between trees and moods: for M/B purposes they are completely of a muchness, and *moods* are the more representative case, rather than the external-world-contingent special case of trees.

To put it another way: it is the relation between feelings and brain states that we are charged with explicating, not the relation between feelings and their *objects*, whether internal or external (i.e., 'feeling that I am seeing a blue balloon' vs. 'feeling [affectively] blue'). *All* such cases are equally symptomatic of and infected with the M/BP; to try instead to resolve some of the differences that distinguish them from one another is just to change the subject and beg the question (and analogous to focussing on differences in notation instead of confronting their common content, except that here it is qualitative content differences that are distracting us from the problem — which is that there exists any content at all!).

> [M]y own view . . . is that the right expression is not so much 'being pained' as 'paining' . . . . sensing is not a passive state at all, but . . . active engagement with the stimulus occurring at the body surface. (p. 13.)

As G.B. Shaw said: 'Madame, we have already established your profession, we are merely haggling about the price.' Call it what one likes — call seeing a tree 'treeseeing', call feeling a pain 'paining' — there is no illumination in sight in this corridor, just gerunds! (The profession here is, unfortunately, question-begging functionalism.)

And let us quickly lay to rest what might have looked as if it too were a contender for a phenomenological category of its own, along with seeing trees vs. feeling pains: performing a volitional act (for example, lifting my finger). No help there either. When I lift my finger, it feels-like 'me-deliberately-finger-lifting'. Just another feeling to account for, along with all the others. The fact that it feels like I'm *doing* it, rather than like it's being *done unto* me, amounts to just one more (irrelevant) difference in feeling content. It does *not* give us any leg up on the M/BP.

Efference is a red herring here. It feels like I'm being the agent, and maybe that's correlated with efferent brain activity: yet another correlation. (Humphrey's proposed 'Sentition' is even worse. We don't need new terms! We need conceptual insights — if there are any to be had.) I, too, happen to have a long-standing interest in the motor component of perception (Harnad, 1982). But there are no inroads to the M/BP from any of that — just perhaps true and interesting functional facts about the relation between afference and efference, reafference, reflexive vs. non-reflexive behaviour, motor theories of perception, etc.

One also cannot agree with Humphrey that 'it is "like something" to have sensations, but not like anything much to engage in most other bodily activities!' (p. 14). Kinaesthesia is qualitative; so is the difference between what it feels like to raise your leg when it has been tapped on the patella by a doctor vs. when you will the motion deliberately. Those are all differences in 'Feeling Space' — just like everything else (including mental imagery and mental reasoning, indeed all of the 'language of thought'). But this casts no light on the M/BP.

Humphrey's 'self-resonance' (p. 15) sounds like just another one in the long litany of 'self-x' terms meant to illuminate consciousness (self-awareness, self-reference, self-representation, etc.) — while in reality merely renaming it.

 (I might add that the 'self' need not figure in it at all: the concept of the 'self' — though, like everything, it has its qualitative contents — surely came late in the evolutionary day. The amphioxus already has a full-blown M/B problem, even though it does not know it, if it aches when you pinch it, and that's the only experience that ever goes on in there — no Cartesian reflection on its being *my* ache and *me* as distinct from *it* as the *patient* of that *sensation*, etc. But just that ache is feeling enough; no 'self-resonance' needed . . . .)

Similarly, the fact that an 'animal has a defining edge to it, a structural boundary' (p. 15) sounds like an excellent functional/Darwinian reason for evolving mechanisms that make the inner–outer distinction, and act upon it. But why should any of that *feel* like anything? Why must one *not* be a *zombie-amoeba* in order to get the full functional benefits Humphrey describes in his evolutionary scenario? (As usual, there is some conflation of the mental and the internal here.)

Organisms 'must evolve the ability to sort out the good from the bad and to respond . . . with an ow' (p.16): Humphrey is here caught in the act of cognistic contraband, smuggling in a *feeling* reaction (otherwise what does the 'ow' mean?), where all that was needed functionally was a *doing* one. Question duly begged.

Similarly with 'When red light falls on it . . . it wriggles redly' (p. 16): why should that *feel* like anything? And if it doesn't, then it's just wriggling wrigglingly, under red conditions. Once one has cheated, and allowed *any* qualitative light to enter into and 'quicken' what should merely have been functional/Darwinian survival/reproduction machines — zombie ones, as plants are [I hope, being a vegetarian who tries not to eat anything that has or has ever had qualia!] — generating the mental stuff one has set out planning to explain, the game is over and the M/B question is begged! Why/how do they wriggle *feelingly* rather than merely *doingly*?

> [A]s yet, these sensory responses are nothing other than responses . . . no reason to suppose that the animal is in any way mentally aware of what is happening. (p. 16.)

A bit of equivocation here: can one be 'aware' in any other way than 'mentally'? And just what is it that is 'happening' if it is not the object of any awareness? If no one is feeling anything, then the events in question might just as well be transpiring on the other side of the moon as within an entity's head, for there is no one home there either. So these are zombies wriggling wrigglingly under red conditions, not wriggling redly. No light means no light, not just paler light.

> [A]s this animal's life becomes more complex, the time comes when it will indeed be advantageous for it to have some kind of inner knowledge of what is affecting it, which it can begin to use as a basis for more sophisticated planning and decision making. So it needs the capacity to form mental representations of the sensory stimulation at the surface of its body and how it feels about it. (p. 16.)

How it *feels* about it? But this was supposed to be the functional explication of what it *is* to feel! In reality, it sounds as if, for functional reasons, the entity needs certain internal structures and processes. Fine, but why should it *feel like* something to have those, or to have them activated (Harnad, 1994)? As before, why/how are these not just zombies with internal structures and processes that do whatever it is that needs functional doing? 'Internal' certainly does not mean 'mental', as every thermostat knows (or rather doesn't).

> By monitoring its own responses, it forms a representation of 'WHAT IS HAPPENING TO ME'. (p. 16.)

We've already settled earlier on the functional utility of an internal distinction between external and internal. But why should *that* feel like anything either? (And if it doesn't, the 'me' has no subject.)

> [W]ouldn't it be better off if, besides being aware of feeling the pressure wave as such (p. 16)

This is again equivocal between functionally-responsive-to the pressure wave and *feeling* it.

> it were able to interpret this stimulus as signalling an approaching predator? (p. 16)

'Interpret' is again equivocal. Functionally, it just means process the information and compute the result. Why should that involve or engender *feelings*?

It should be clear by now that Humphrey has got out of this exactly what he has put into it. His language and caveats are equivocal about precisely where, how, or why he has smuggled in the light of consciousness (or the warmth of feelings), but clearly at some point he has, and we are meant to go along with this.

Alas, I cannot, because Humphrey has given me no reason — functional or logical — for doing so. He has simply arbitrarily turned on the mental lights at some juncture, and somehow attributed that to the Darwinian story he was telling; yet the story (except as a Just-So story, i.e., as mere hermeneutics) does not explain or justify it at all.

> When the question is 'what is happening to me?', the answer that is wanted is qualitative, present-tense, transient, and subjective. When the question is 'what is happening out there?', the answer that is wanted is quantitative, analytical, permanent, and objective. (p. 17.)

No account whatsoever is given of why this should be the case. Why do internal data have to have the mental lights on, whereas external data do not? (I don't even think it's true, in that external-object-event-processing is probably just as closely correlated with consciousness as internal.)

It is conceivable that two systems evolved along the lines Humphrey describes; it is even conceivable that there are some correlations between his functional account and consciousness (although even functionally some parts seem problematic).

But the part Humphrey owes us, if this is really meant to have any bearing on the M/B problem, is an explanation of when/how/why *feelings* kicked in (whatever their correlation with these two hypothetical systems might be).

> [P]roto-experience of sensation arises from its monitoring its own command signals for these sensory responses. (p. 17.)

'Proto' is a weasel word here: are we talking about feelings, or about something else? I do not know, nor can I conceive, of anything intermediate or 'proto' in between feeling and non-feeling. And it would be sensation when the mental lights went on, not 'experience of sensation', which is redundant. With the mental lights off, sensation is just 'event' or 'physical effect' or 'response'. Optical transducers respond to light; they don't have sensations. There's no one in there to be the subject of sensations, to feel; and sensations are experiences, feelings, full-blown. (Self-monitoring is an old favourite. But why *feelingly* self-monitoring, rather than *zombily*?)

> [T]hough the animal may no longer want to respond directly to the stimulation at its body surface as such, it still wants to be able to keep up to date mentally with what's occurring. (p. 17.)

Delays, planning, monitoring, policing: all good stuff, and we ourselves all certainly do it mentally; but that's neither here nor there. How/why is it mental rather than just internal but mindless zombie adaptation here, in this putative explication? (These are the *hard* questions.) In his functional account, Humphrey has described some very useful internal computations, but he has left out entirely how/why they have anything feelingful about them. Till he can do that, the M/BP has been untouched by any of this.

Humphrey's closed-circuits and internal loops are also popular candidates for 'self-x' structures/processes (self-modifying and self-organizing are others), but all of these are too easy! One cannot just baptize them as 'mental' and declare that a problem has been solved. It is the simplest thing (and indeed valid, because of the M/B correlation) to give a mentalistic interpretation to certain brain processes. But to *interpret* them as mental (even *truly* so) is not to *explain* them (causally) as mental! Such are the limits of mentalistic hermeneutics (Harnad, 1990a,b).

> Now once this happens, [natural] selection is no longer involved in determining the form of these responses and . . . the quality of the representations based on them. (p. 18.)

This is a reasonable rationale for replacing further evolutionary adaptation by all-purpose learning and intelligence, based on evolved internal cognitive mechanisms, but not a hint about why/how any of this is conscious (Harnad, 2000).

I never quite figured out what Humphrey's 'thickness factor' was (perhaps there was something intentionally Geertzian about it [Geertz, 1973]) — apart from the fact that it appears to be making some sort of a continuum out of something that is all or none: either feeling is going on or it is not; if it is, then we are again just haggling about the price; but Humphrey owes us an explanation of how/why the feeling-switch was turned on at all in the first place.

> when the process becomes internalized and the circuit so much shortened, the conditions are there for a significant degree of recursive interaction to come into play . . . the command signals for sensory responses begin to loop back upon themselves, becoming in the process partly self-creating and self-sustaining . . . they have . . . become signals about themselves. (p. 19.)

I can design and implement recursive, self-sustaining loops fitting Humphrey's description easily. Do they quicken with the light of consciousness too? If not, then why/how do the ones Humphrey says do, do? Animating the 'self-x' words does not explain, it covers up! And it's not getting signals that are 'about' themselves that is the problem — for this very sentence is now about itself too; the problem is getting someone in there for those signals to be about something *to*: a conscious subject. That problem is hard and, alas, Nick Humphrey, like everyone else so far, has failed to solve it.

References

Chalmers, D. (1996), *The Conscious Mind* (Oxford: Oxford University Press).

Geertz, C. (1973), *The Interpretation of Cultures; Selected Essays* (New York, Basic Books).

Harnad, S. (1982), 'Consciousness: An afterthought', *Cognition and Brain Theory*, 5, pp. 29–47, http://www.cogsci.soton.ac.uk/~harnad/Papers/Harnad/harnad82.consciousness.html.

Harnad, S. (1990a), 'Against computational hermeneutics', Invited commentary on Eric Dietrich's Computationalism, *Social Epistemology*, 4, pp. 167–72, http://www.cogsci.soton.ac.uk/~harnad/Papers/Harnad/harnad90.dietrich.crit.html.

Harnad, S. (1990b), 'Lost in the hermeneutic hall of mirrors', Invited Commentary on Michael Dyer: Minds, Machines, Searle and Harnad. *Journal of Experimental and Theoretical Artificial Intelligence*, 2, pp. 321–7, http://www.cogsci.soton.ac.uk/~harnad/Papers/Harnad/harnad90.dyer.crit.html.

Harnad, S. (1994), 'Levels of functional equivalence in reverse bioengineering: The Darwinian Turing test for artificial life', *Artificial Life*, 1(3), pp. 293–301, reprinted in *Artificial Life: An Overview*, ed. C.G. Langton (MIT Press, 1995), http://www.cogsci.soton.ac.uk/~harnad/Papers/Harnad/harnad94.artlife2.html.

Harnad, S. (1995), 'Why and how we are not zombies', *Journal of Consciousness Studies*, 1, pp. 164–7, http://www.cogsci.soton.ac.uk/~harnad/Papers/Harnad/harnad95.zombies.html.

Harnad, S. (2000), 'Turing indistinguishability and the blind watchmaker', in *Evolving Consciousness*, ed. G. Mulhauser and J. Fetzer (Amsterdam: John Benjamins), http://www.cogsci.soton.ac.uk/~harnad/Papers/Harnad/harnad98.turing.evol.html.

Harnad, S. (2001), 'Minds, machines, and Turing: The indistinguishability of indistinguishables', *Journal of Logic, Language, and Information*, special issue on 'Alan Turing and Artificial Intelligence' (in press), http://www.cogsci.soton.ac.uk/~harnad/Papers/Harnad/harnad00.turing.html.

Humphrey, N. (2000), 'How to solve the mind–body problem', *Journal of Consciousness Studies*, 7 (4), pp. 5–20 (this issue).

McGinn, C. (1989), 'Can we solve the mind–body problem?', *Mind*, 98, pp. 349–66.

Nagel, T. (1974), 'What is like to be a bat?', *Philosophical Review*, 83, pp. 435–51.

Nagel, T. (1986), *The View From Nowhere* (New York: Oxford University Press).

Natika Newton

Humphrey's Solution

I: Introduction

It is easy to conceptualize a problem in a way that prevents a solution. If the conceptualization is entrenched in one's culture or profession, it may appear unalterable. But there is so much precedent for the discovery of fruitful reconceptualizations that in the case of most philosophical and scientific puzzles it is probably irrational ever to give up trying. The notion of qualia, understood as phenomenal properties of sensations that can exist as objects of experience for a conscious subject, is too recent in origin and too specialized in usage to warrant concluding that qualia cannot be understood in terms of physical processes. Humphrey (2000) offers an analysis of qualitative mental states that purportedly renders them commensurate with brain states, allowing them to be described in terms of the same dimensions. If his attempt is successful the conceptual gap between mind and body could be closed. Is it successful?

I argue that it comes extremely close, but that the attempt is less convincing than it could be because the language of the proposed analysis in some places remains that of the tradition Humphrey seeks to replace. His contribution is important because he has left only a few steps to a complete reconceptualization of qualitative mental states. In this commentary, after explaining the objections, I will offer a sketch of how those steps might be taken.

II: Summary of Humphrey's View

Humphrey argues that mental and physical states seem incommensurable because mental states, conceived as sensations, are described as if they are the *objects* of experience. In fact, however, they are *activities*: sensings of the true objects: physical stimuli with which the organism is actively engaged. Conceiving of sensations as themselves objects of experience (and then talking, as so many do, of what that experience 'is like') leads to a hopeless regress. There is no 'mental object' corresponding to 'experience', and any proposed candidate for it immediately becomes itself the source of more mysterious 'objects': the 'phenomenal properties of experiences' which are themselves 'like something', *ad infinitum*.

As long as sensations are conceived of as non-physical objects that can be experienced, they cannot be explained in terms of brain states, objects of a completely different metaphysical kind. Humphrey's first move is to distinguish between perception and sensation, and to point out that while perception is indeed 'of' external physical objects, sensations are not mental objects of an 'inner sense'; instead,

Journal of Consciousness Studies, **7**, No. 4, 2000, pp. 62–6

'sensory awareness is an activity. We do not have pains, we get to be pained' (p. 13). Sensory awareness is efferent activity, and the experience it provides is not the experience of a mental object, a sensation, but the experience of the activity itself. In his second move, Humphrey argues that sensory activity has evolved from responses that in the past did carry through into actual behaviour. And the result is that, even today, the experience of sensation retains many of the original characteristics of true bodily action (p. 13).

Explaining sensory activity in terms of bodily activity allows Humphrey to correlate it with brain activity. Sensation, like bodily action, is characterized by: ownership, bodily location, presentness, qualitative modality, and phenomenal immediacy. Each of these can be understood in terms of brain states, because they are 'dual currency concepts', neither purely mental nor purely physical. Humphrey concludes with a plausible evolutionary scenario that would connect the two sides of the mind–body problem.

III: An Objection

Humphrey's proposal is that sensation is analogous to bodily activity, and that the reason for this is that the activity of sensing evolved from the bodily activities of responding to stimuli. He holds that the experiences characteristic of sensation are analysable in terms of properties of bodily activity itself: activities are owned, activities have distinct modalities (*hand* waves, *knee* jerks), etc. He carefully acknowledges a disanalogy: 'it is "like something" to have sensations, but not like anything much to engage in most other activities' (p. 14). He accounts for the disanalogy by arguing that sensations are self-resonating, and hence possess a temporal 'thickness' that sets them apart and makes them more vivid.

There is a confusion in the above account. There is indeed an analogy between sensation and action, but Humphrey has compared the wrong aspects of them. For him, the analogy lies between the objective features of action and the subjective features of sensation. But he overlooks the fact that every one of the objective features of action that he cites is also subjectively sensed, even in a context of pure action. This confusion is evident in his remark that it is like something to have sensations but not to engage in most other activities. It may be that we tend to focus conscious attention most strongly on sensations that are linked to objects in the external world (sight, hearing, taste, etc.). But that is not the same as saying that it is not like much to engage in other activities. Moving one's foot, even while not looking at it, can be a vivid experience. More important, if our bodily activities were not experienced as sensations, as 'like something' for us to at least the same degree as other sensations, we would be unable to experience the latter in many of the dimensions he lists. This claim is defended in the following section.

IV: Arguments for the Primacy of Bodily Activity in Experience

There are at least three ways the above claim can be supported. First, let us look at Humphrey's defining properties of sensation. Consider ownership. Sensation, he says, 'always belongs to the subject'. His example is pain, but it could have been visual sensations instead. If Humphrey had picked visual sensations, however, his point would not have been so obvious. Visual sensations do not *feel* like sensations;

instead, sensations like colour appear to a naïve subject to be properties of external objects (Newton, 1989; Ellis and Newton, 1998). Sound, to a lesser degree, also appears to the average listener to exist at the source of the sound waves rather than in our bodies. The same can be said of Humphrey's second property of the experience of sensation: bodily location. Pain is again too easy an example: seeing a red object does not 'intrinsically involve *this* part of *me*'. There is normally no felt sensation in the eyes when we see red.

If sensations such as red,[1] which appear 'velvety and thick' (p. 14), are owned and indexical in the way that pain is, that is because the bodily activities involved in see-ing an external object are equally velvety and thick. They may not be the primary focus of conscious attention, but they are integral to the visual experience. In seeing a red apple, I cannot help but see it as something *in front of me*, as *reachable and grasp-able by me*, or else as out of *my reach*. It is seen, as many have noted following Gib-son, in terms of its *affordances*. Its affordances are the various ways that it does and can interact with my body. If I can see an object only in this way, then my body in its current state is part of the visual experience. To see something, but not see it as an object in front of one's eyes, is difficult if not impossible to imagine.

The second argument that our bodily activities are vividly experienced is more direct: they underlie our ongoing sense of self as agency. Without a sense of self as acting in the world, sensations of external objects would be meaningless. More important, bodily sensations not only provide a context for other sensations, but they often successfully compete with them for attention. Of course I can forget myself in watching an absorbing movie. But normally my attention is not so securely captured, and I pay attention to my actions, evaluate my current bodily state, consider how my actions may appear to others, or am simply reminded by bodily sensations of my exis-tence. Even in the movie, I frequently remember that 'it is only a movie' that *I am watching*. There have been proposals recently that the ongoing sense of self is medi-ated by continual processing of information about the current state of the body. Panksepp (1998) argues that this processing is located primarily in parts of the upper brain stem such as the periaquaductal grey region. It may also involve conscious awareness of efference copy (corollary discharge): copies of motor commands sent to other processing areas of the brain, such as the basal ganglia and the cerebellum, which return processed signals to the cortical motor areas (Hurley, 1998; Zigmond *et al.*, 1999). It should be noted that voluntary direction of attention is also a bodily activity of which we can be aware.

Finally, there has been a surge of interest in recent years in the experience of 'em-bodiment' as underlying cognition in general. Examples are numerous (see, for example, Boden, 1982; Clark, 1997; Jackendoff, 1987; Lakoff and Johnson, 1987; Langacker, 1987; Newton, 1996; Sheets-Johnstone, 1998). The common theme is that cognition at all levels of abstraction makes essential use of images of basic bodily actions, and that such action schemas constitute the framework for all concep-tual domains, including mathematics and logic. Supporting this view is work by Jeannerod (1994; 1997) showing that action images are essential for performing vol-untary action, and that they are consciously accessible. If this new thinking is sound,

---

[1] Humphrey reverts to colour sensations when he no longer needs to emphasize their relation to the sub-ject's body.

then experiences of bodily action are far from 'flat and papery' (Humphrey, p. 14); instead, they constitute the experienced building materials of our conscious life.

V: Significance of the Objection for Humphrey's Argument

In treating the experience of bodily activity as weak and peripheral, and arguing that other sensations are richer because they evolved from bodily responses to stimuli, Humphrey renders his position vulnerable to empirical refutation in a way that should be actually irrelevant. Evidence that sensations are not 'privatized' bodily responses (p. 18) would seriously undermine his argument. Part of his empirical claim, at least, is weak. Why, if sensations are privatized physical responses, are they therefore more 'velvety and thick' than current physical activities? Humphrey explains this as a result of the 'shortening' of the sensory response pathway, but the explanation is extremely brief and sketchy, and cites no empirical studies. If instead he were to grant that sensations of bodily activity are experienced in the same way as sensations of external objects, then the evolutionary scenario, plausible though it might be, would be irrelevant. The real issue would then become the 'thickness factor'. *All* sensings are subject to recursive interaction; all sensings, externally or internally (imagistically) generated, are subject to internal loops that create a 'self-resonance', allowing the sensing activity itself to appear as an 'object' of experience. This is true as much for our experience of bodily action as for exteroception. Any ongoing conscious experience requires working memory for retention of immediately preceding states, which resonate with similar current states. Self-resonance is possible not because a sensation is a mental rather than a physical entity, but because the activity of sensing is experienced like any other activity. A sense of ownership is provided by the experience of agency and an egocentric perspective on the sensed objects in the world, including one's own physical body. Feedback loops create a present experience of blended self and world, extended by memory and anticipation, providing the present moment of efferent sensory activity with an *illusory solidity and substance* that we find mysterious, but whose explanation may actually turn out to be quite straightforward.

VI: Conclusion

Humphrey's article contains some profound insights. The most important ones are that sensations are activities, and that the 'thick moment of consciousness' can be analysed in terms of physical mechanisms to provide a bridge between mind and body. This latter idea especially, which goes back at least to William James, has never been adequately investigated. I hope that this aspect of Humphrey's theory will be pursued, both empirically and conceptually. It has the potential to bridge the explanatory gap; no competing theory comes close.

References

Boden, M. (1982), 'Implications of language studies for human nature', in *Language, Mind and Brain*, ed. Simon and Scholes (Hillsdale, NJ: Lawrence Erlbaum).

Clark, A. (1997), *Being There* (Cambridge, MA: MIT Press).

Ellis, R. and Newton, N. (1998), 'Three paradoxes of phenomenal consciousness', *Journal of Consciousness Studies*, **5** (4), pp. 419–42.

Humphrey, N. (2000), 'How to solve the mind–body problem', *Journal of Consciousness Studies*, **7** (4), pp. 5–20 (this issue).

Hurley, S. (1998), *Consciousness in Action* (Cambridge, MA: Harvard University Press).

Jackendoff, R. (1987), *Conscious and the Computational Mind* (Cambridge, MA: MIT Press).

Lakoff, G. and Johnson, M. (1987), *Women, Fire and Dangerous Things* (Chicago: University of Chicago Press).

Langacker, R. (1987), T*he Foundations of Cognitive Grammar Vol. 1* (Stanford: Stanford University Press).

Newton, N. (1989), 'On viewing pain as a secondary quality', *NOUS*, **23** (5), pp. 569–98.

Newton, N. (1996), *Foundations of Understanding* (Amsterdam: John Benjamins).

Panksepp, J. (1998), 'The periconscious substrates of consciousness: Affective states and the evolutionary origins of the self', *Journal of Consciousness Studies*, **5** (5–6), pp. 566–83.

Sheets-Johnstone, M. (1998), 'Consciousness: A natural history', *Journal of Consciousness Studies*, **5** (3), pp. 260–94.

Zigmond, M., Bloom, F., Landis, S., Roberts, J., Squire, L. (1999), *Fundamental Neuroscience* (New York: Academic Press).

Christian de Quincey

Conceiving the 'Inconceivable'?

Fishing for Consciousness with a Net of Miracles

Sometimes, after years of painstaking work, someone presents a startling argument that seems to suddenly snatch the ground right out from under your feet. And it's back to square one.

Such a conceptual trapdoor caught me by surprise a few years ago. For decades, I had been convinced it is simply *inconceivable* that subjectivity — the interior experience of how consciousness *feels* — could possibly emerge from a previously wholly objective world, that mind could evolve from 'dead' matter. It seemed to me that the arguments of materialist philosophers, cognitive scientists and neuroscientists invariably missed the point. They always began with an assumption of ontological objectivity or physicality, and proceeded to show that *that* must be the source of consciousness. Well, of course, it had to be — given their starting assumption. But what they were talking about wasn't consciousness at all. It was usually either some neural correlation, some computer analogue, or some complex and abstract linguistic deconstruction. Whatever their approach, the first-person experience of consciousness — it's subjective *feel* — always slipped through their grasp. They were looking at the problem from the third-person perspective — from objectivity. And you can't get to here (subjectivity) from there.

Or so I believed. Then I happened to read Nicholas Humphrey's *A History of the Mind* (1992), where he presented a clear and plausible argument for a materialist account of consciousness and subjectivity. Not only was I struck by the literacy of his style, and the easy accessibility of his ideas, I found that as he led me through the step-by-step logic of his theory, I could see no obvious point where his reasoning was flawed. When I finished the book I realized that even if his theory were incomplete or wrong — even if his particular model of how mind emerged from matter turns out to be factually in error — I was still left with the uncomfortable realization that the mere existence of such a theory meant the previously inconceivable was now, at the very least, conceivable (even if it wasn't true). My favourite ontological thesis — variously called panpsychism, panexperientialism, or radical naturalism — was in real trouble.

Although my prior conviction was shaken, intuitively I was sure Humphrey must be wrong. I read his book a second time searching for the fatal flaw. The underlying premise of radical naturalism (and of panpsychism and panexperientialism) is the notion — no, the *assertion* — that mind cannot emerge from wholly insentient

Journal of Consciousness Studies, **7**, No. 4, 2000, pp. 67–81

matter. If the world began as wholly objective matter–energy, without even a mini-mal trace of subjectivity, then there is no conceivable way that first-person experi-ence could ever emerge in the cosmos. The universe would always and forever be unexperienced and unknown. It would never contain a point of view, not even a 'view from nowhere', to use Thomas Nagel's (1986) famous and evocative phrase. There would be no point of view, period.

Yet very clearly and definitely the world does contain a point of view — there *is* a view from 'here'. Following the lead of Campanella and Descartes, I can be certain of one thing: I am thinking, I am conscious, I am experiencing, I know what it feels like to be me. In short, I have a subjective point of view. That is certain. And, since I am not inclined to solipsism, I am willing to bet that you, too, have a point of view. In fact, I am willing to bet that the universe is populated with countless billions of view-points. Subjectivity is an indisputable fact.

Given this fact, and the premise of the inconceivability of subjectivity arising from pure objectivity, I am compelled to conclude that the universe could not *ever* have been *purely* objective. There must have been, *always*, something of the nature of sub-jectivity inherent in the universe. This is the lynch-pin of my thesis of 'radical natu-ralism' — that the raw 'stuff' of nature, its primordial 'matter,' must have always possessed an 'interiority' (Wilber), a 'within' (de Chardin), an 'occasion of experi-ence' (Whitehead), a quantum of consciousness (Young), a capacity for a subjective viewpoint (Nagel), a self-organizing 'intelligence' (Bruno).

If this foundational premise of 'inconceivability' were to be removed, the entire edifice of radical naturalism and panexperientialism would come tumbling down.

It was therefore a great surprise for me to discover Humphrey's account of 'How to Solve the Mind–Body Problem' — presented in *A History of the Mind* and again in this issue of *JCS* with an even more explicit materialist assertion: '*mental state, m = brain state, b*' — mind is *identical* to brain.

Humphrey bravely sets out to show why both sides of the equation are identical in kind. His strategy is to focus on the 'mind' side, and persuade us that its origins and development share precisely the same characteristics that apply to the 'brain' side. It's a straightforward, no-nonsense strategy, and of all materialist mind–brain theo-ries, I find his the most compelling, coherent, and challenging. Of course, his strategy would backfire if he fails to make a watertight case that the left side of the equation, mind, is in fact identical in type to what we believe we know about the right side, mat-ter. In this response, I will examine in some detail Humphrey's attempt to trace the physical basis of mind to roots in wholly non-mental nature, and see whether he suc-ceeds in his stated aim of setting out '*the [mind–brain] identity in a way that meets certain minimum standards for explanatory possibility*' (Humphrey, 2000, p. 7). In short, does he provide the needed explanation, or does he slip in a miracle along the way?

However, in order to show just how seductive and persuasive his theory is — to let you feel its full impact — I will need to explore some of the conceptual background that didn't make it into his *JCS* article — points that are essential, I believe, for fully appreciating the attraction of his evolutionary model of consciousness. I will outline the genesis of his crucial theory of the 'extended present' (1992) or of the 'thickened moment' (1995), as he variously calls it, and show why in the end I think it doesn't succeed — precisely at the point where he must either call on some form of panpsych-ism or resort to a miracle.

What caught my attention from the start was Humphrey's recognition that, to succeed, any such theory must address the problem of getting *subjectivity from wholly non-subjective raw materials* (Humphrey, 1992). He had zoomed right in on the critical issue.

Humphrey is convinced that consciousness is a result of a series of physical and biological events in evolution — events that led to the *emergence of mind from mindless matter*. He is clearly aware that for such emergence to occur there cannot be an ontological jump from one kind of reality to a wholly different kind. Mind or subjectivity must be of the same ontological *type* as matter or objectivity — 'both sides [of the equation] must represent the same *kind* of thing' (Humphrey, 2000, p. 8). And further, quoting A.S. Ramsey approvingly, it must be the same kind of '*physical* thing'.

I think Humphrey is correct to insist on the requirement of ontological equivalency: Mind and brain must be tokens of the same ontological type. Any jump from one ontological type to another would involve fatally problematic dualism, and would require the intrusion of a miracle. But I think his insistence on the single type being *physical* forces him in the end, also, to need a miracle for his mind–brain equation to work — unless he radically redefines 'physical' so that it includes subjectivity, sentience, or consciousness all the way down (de Quincey, 1994), and switches from a substance-based ontology to a process one (de Quincey, 1999).

The following summary will condense the main steps in his argument outlined in *A History of the Mind* and abbreviated in this issue. Here, I am interested only in the salient links in his chain of logic. I will not be able to fill in all the details, and I urge anyone interested in exploring Humphrey's theory to read his book. It is short, easy going, and rewarding for anyone interested in the perennial issue of the mind–body relation.

He starts with the big picture, the grand evolutionary sweep, which means going back to the creation of the Earth (and even earlier), because, as he says, he wishes 'to make no preliminary assumptions about when mind and consciousness emerged', and also 'to make no assumptions about objective reality'. On the first point, he says:

> I take it for granted that the human mind does indeed have an evolutionary history, extending through non-human prototypes — monkeys, reptiles, worms — all the way back to the first glimmerings of life on Earth.

And on the second point:

> Before life emerged, let's say four billion years ago, when the planet Earth was formed, there were presumably no minds at all. It follows that four billion years ago the world was totally unexperienced and unknown (Humphrey, 1992, p. 38).

So, on point one, he is with the panexperientialists in assuming that consciousness goes back a long way, even to the first flourishings of life. In other words, like panexperientialists (and unlike many biologists), he does not assume that consciousness *per se* is an emergent property of higher brains and nervous systems. Something of the quality of human consciousness is to be found way back, even in single-celled creatures. And this 'quality', of course, is nothing like introspective thought, or self-reflective feelings. It is something much more primitive, what he calls 'consciousness as raw sensation' (1992, p. 18), or 'what it is like to experience consciousness from the inside' (1992, p. 25), or his current favourite (from Newton) 'sensory phantasms' (2000, p. 10).

With this definition, then, we know from the start that he is talking about consciousness as subjectivity, not merely the psychoanalyst's 'conscious' (as contrasted

with the 'unconscious'), or the neuroscientist's neural correlates of mind, or the functionalist's or AI theorist's computer-simulated algorithms of mental operations such
as computational thinking or symbol generation and syntax. That's what piqued my
interest in the first chapter of his book: He was out to catch and to fry the very same
'fish'[1] that I have been after all these years. He was after 'subjective feeling', and he
wanted to account for intentionality, meaning, and qualia, too. (In the *JCS* article he
downplays the usefulness of the term 'qualia', and prefers synonyms such as 'phenomenal consciousness', and, more simply, 'sensation'. As we shall see, 'sensation'
turns out to be the all-important ingredient in his mind–brain identity theory.)

But on point two, he broke rank with the panexperientialists when he assumed (as
any self-respecting materialist would) that before life appeared on Earth, there was
no such thing even resembling mind at all. When the planet formed 'the world was
totally unexperienced and unknown', and had been that way for the eleven or so billion years since the Big Bang. (So, despite what he says, he *does* make an assumption
about 'objective reality'.) Taking the original meaning of 'phenomenon' (from the
Greek *phainein*, 'to appear') — that is, 'an event as it appears to an observer, as distinguished from what it might consist of in itself' — he says of the Big Bang, that
whatever it was like, 'there was no phenomenal bang at the time it occurred'. At the
Big Bang, there was no observer, no subjective point of view, therefore there was no
phenomenon. There was only the raw physical event (which, of course, we can only
infer because we now exist as experiencing subjects, to whom the residual
three-degree background radiation — the faint 'echo' of the Big Bang — is *now* a
phenomenon). Back then, there only was the raw 'is'.

Getting Wine from Water?

But between then and now, we know that consciousness did appear. The big question
is '*How?*' Humphrey lays out the central problem of the mind–matter mystery in
terms of the human mind–brain puzzle. He lists three facts:

(1) We experience subjective feelings, which are beyond description in purely phys-
     ical terms. Phenomena such as 'pain' are not a part of the objective world. They
     belong to a *first-person point of view*.
(2) Subjective phenomena, such as the pain felt when we bite our tongue, are related
     to processes going on in our brains. These processes are describable in the objec-
     tive language of physics and chemistry. They are accessible from a *third-person
     point of view*.
(3) So far as we know, he says, 'Fact 1 wholly depends on Fact 2. In other words, the
     subjective feeling is brought about by the brain processes' (1992, p. 25). And it is
     this third fact — the mind–body relation — that has been inexplicable by science
     and philosophy ever since the problem was noticed.

Faced with this mystery, the great British evolutionist T.H. Huxley said:

> How it is that anything so remarkable as a state of consciousness comes about as a result
> of irritating nerve tissue is just as unaccountable as the appearance of the Djinn, where
> Aladdin rubbed his lamp . . . (quoted in McGinn, 1991, p. 99).

---

[1] Humphrey employs the metaphor of catching a fish to indicate his approach to coaxing consciousness
     out of its hidden lair in evolution: 'I believe the way to catch consciousness will be to tickle it. That is to
     say we should discover where it is lying, approach it slowly, and then charm it into our hands' (1992,
     p. 37).

And Colin McGinn expressed a similar sense of cognitive defeat:

> Somehow, we feel, the water of the physical brain is turned into the wine of consciousness, but we draw a total blank on the nature of this conversion. . . . The mind–body problem is the problem of understanding how the miracle is wrought (McGinn, 1994, pp. 99–100).

Invoking or materializing the *Djinn*, and turning water into wine require magic if not miracle. Getting consciousness from 'the dark foam of insensate matter', as Humphrey poetically calls it (1992, p. 23), has seemed to many philosophers and scientists to require no less of a miracle. It is what I have been calling 'the inconceivable'. But having rejected the panexperientialist position by assuming that in the beginning the universe consisted only of insensate matter, and given his 'Fact 1', Humphrey is convinced that such a 'miracle' *must* have, in fact, occurred. Of course, he is intent on arguing that it was not at all a miraculous event, but something wholly natural, wholly explicable by normal materialist science.

He makes his physicalist bias quite clear: 'They — we [cognitive scientists] — all assume that the human mind and brain are . . . aspects of a single state — a single state, in fact, of the material world, which in principle could be fully described in terms of its microphysical components' (2000, p. 5); and 'The first task of a theory of consciousness has to be to . . . describe a physical process in the brain whose properties, at the appropriate level of description, correspond to the properties of felt sensations' (1992, p. 202). Precisely such a description is what Humphrey claims to deliver.

Here's how he structures the components of his theory. I'll identify four major elements, each of which involves its own chain of argument. The major elements are (1) The importance of boundaries; (2) The distinction between sensation and perception; (3) Sensations are 'instructions'; and (4) The thick moment of the extended present.

The Importance of Boundaries

Humphrey begins *History* by declaring 'Everything that is interesting in nature happens at the boundaries: the surface of the Earth, the membrane of a cell, the moment of catastrophe, the start and finish of a life' (1992, p. 23). He builds his theory as follows:

One — no boundaries. In the beginning, the Big Bang was a wholly physical event, wholly non-subjective. (He wouldn't use 'wholly objective' because, as he rightly notes, something can only be objective if there exists a subjective point of view to contrast it with. Since there was no subjectivity, strictly speaking there was no objectivity either. There just was 'is'.) In the initial moments after the Big Bang the emerging universe was completely chaotic, an amorphous plasma of interfused 'particles' and radiation. There was no distinctiveness or separateness to speak of. No individuality. No distinction between 'here' and 'there', no 'inside' or 'outside', and certainly no 'self' or 'other'. Although a buzzing chaos of light-speed activity and interacting forces, the universe was 'dead', intrinsically inert and meaningless.

Two — physical boundaries emerge. After billions of years of cosmic expansion and progressive cooling of the universe, individual particles, atoms and molecules had formed. As a result of chemical evolution in the hearts of stars, matter began to settle down, stabilizing as chemical elements. Planets, rich with complex chemical ingredients, formed, and from these ingredients, a primeval soup brewed under intense solar and cosmic radiation.

Three — chemical boundaries and self-replication emerge. Through the action of chance collisions of molecules in the primordial soup, the first molecules capable of making copies of themselves happened to form. The first raw materials of life, 'packets of worldstuff' (p. 39), emerged with an increasing capacity for maintaining the integrity of their boundaries, and improving their capacity for reproduction.

Four — biological boundaries emerge. Simple 'packets' of self-replicating molecules, wrapped up in the protective sheath of a semi-permeable membrane form the first primitive cells. These 'creatures' are able to actively control the passage of information and energy across their membrane — the boundary separating what is 'inside' from what is 'outside'. The evolution of membranes, primitive 'skin', was crucial for the maintenance of life, and would be the deciding factor in the emergence of mind.

Five — discriminating boundaries/selective membranes. The appearance of semi-permeable biological boundaries gave rise to the first distinction between 'inside' and 'outside' and between 'self' and 'other'.[2] These membranes, capable of allowing some external material in, while keeping other stuff out, and also capable of maintaining an optimal internal state of cooperation among its self-replicating chemicals and between these and the membrane, gave rise to the first distinction between what was 'good' or 'bad' for the organism. Anything that enhanced survival and reproductive ability was 'good', anything that threatened these was 'bad'.

Six — Natural selection kicks in and favours *sensitivity*. Through chance variations in the replicating mechanism, some copies of the original organisms would have developed membranes with greater selectivity or sensitivity to discriminate between 'good' and 'bad' stimuli impacting on the organism's surface. Evolution would, therefore, favour those organisms that developed a greater sensitivity for discrimination because they would have improved survival and reproductive 'fitness'.

Seven — Natural selection favours flexibility of *response*. Again through the processes of chance variations and natural selection, some organisms would improve their 'sensitivity', that is, their ability to react selectively at the location where the stimulus occurred. A greater repertoire of reactive responses, such as retraction of the surface away from 'bad' stimuli, or expanding the surface to engulf 'good' stimuli, would further enhance differential survival and reproductive fitness.

Eight — Natural selection favours *non-local reactivity*. Organisms that developed the ability to *delay* and *displace* their responses, so that they didn't always immediately react at the spot on the surface where the stimuli impinged, would lead to increased flexibility of responses, and improved adaptive fitness. With the evolution of nervous systems, organisms could relay information from one part of the surface to other parts. Such displaced reactivity would amount to a *delay* in the organism's response.

------

[2] This is an interesting aspect of Humphrey's theory. The distinction between 'inside' and 'outside', based on a *physical* boundary, is the source of the distinction between 'self' and 'other'. Now, as critics of materialist ontologies (such as Ken Wilber, 1995) point out, there is a world of difference between 'inside' (meaning a physical location) and 'interior' (meaning a non-spatial experiential dimension). To equate the two is to collapse a fundamental ontological distinction. However, since it is precisely Humphrey's stated aim that the flat-level ontology of materialism is sufficient to account for subjectivity and consciousness, one of his first tasks is to show how 'inside' (within a physical boundary) is, in fact, the origin of the sensation or experience of 'interiority' and 'self'. If he succeeds in this, his theory poses a serious challenge to panexperientialism/radical naturalism and idealism.

Nine — Natural selection favours *affective reactions*. Discrimination between 'good' and 'bad' stimuli, coupled with an ability to move toward or away from the stimuli (with variations of these responses) amounts to 'liking' what is good for 'me' (the bounded individual) and 'disliking' what is bad for 'me'. Using words 'like' and 'dislike' indicates the presence of 'affect' or discriminatory sensitivity or 'feelings' and, therefore, the appearance of proto-mentality.

The introduction of 'like' and 'dislike' is justified because the surface discrimination/sensitivity implies a *preference* for good over bad stimuli. Further, 'like' also implies a preference for *self-similar* stimuli or objects because they can be assimilated through the membrane, and more easily incorporated in the internal activities of the cell. The organism likes (selects/prefers) what is like itself (self-similar). And, from another perspective, to like (prefer) what is like (self-similar) implies that there is something it is *like* to be the *subject* within the self-boundary (subjectivity).

Thus, at stage nine, we already have the basic ingredients for mind or consciousness: We have *subjectivity* within the bounded individual; we have *feeling* at the surface where the selectivity between incoming stimuli amounts to sensitivity; we have *affect* also at the surface where the variations in response patterns (moving toward or away) amounts to *preference* or unconscious choice between 'like' and 'dislike'; we have *meaning* and *intentionality* where events at the surface are discriminated as either 'good' or 'bad' for '*me*' (that is, the internal structure and dynamics of the membrane-encapsulated individual). Discriminatory sensitivity (sensory affect) based on distinctions or 'preferences' for 'good' or 'bad' stimuli is, therefore, the basis of what later comes to be called 'consciousness' or 'experience'.[3]

Ten — Delayed reaction patterns require stored representations, and that means *mind*. With the evolution of displaced or non-local reactions to local stimuli, responses are *delayed*, and to some extent decoupled, from sensitivity. This means, in effect, that a 'central site evolved, where representation — in the form of action patterns — were held in abeyance before they were put into effect. . . . The place where they were held in store could be said to be the place where they were held in mind' (1992, p. 42). Humphrey goes on to say,

> In short, animals first had 'minds' when they first became capable of storing — and possibly recalling and reworking — action-based representations of the effects of environmental stimulation on their own bodies. The material substrate of the mind was nervous tissue. . . . The neural tube which forms the brain during embryological development derives from an infolding of the skin (1992, p. 42).

If Humphrey's theory of mind emerging from wholly insensate matter, and of subjectivity emerging from 'objectivity', is plausible, then already the radical naturalist thesis of panexperientialism based on the 'inconceivability' of such emergence is seriously weakened. But this is only the start. Humphrey goes on to lay out in clear detail many more elements of his theory.

Thus far, his theory claims to account only for the phenomenon of subjectivity, for how an animal can answer the question 'What is happening to me?' or 'What something is like for me?' But the theory does not yet explain how the animal could account for 'what is happening out there?' — for the external location or source of the

---

[3] Humphrey emphasizes that unless and until psychology reinstates the central role of 'sensory affect', the sense of enjoyment, of pleasure and pain — which William Drummond in 1623 called 'the organs of delight' — psychology will go on 'fishing for consciousness in an empty pool' (p. 51).

incoming stimuli. And such an ability is of paramount importance. When an animal doesn't have to wait until a stimulus makes physical contact with its skin — for example, the feeling of a hawk's talons gripping the skin of a rabbit — the animal's survival will be significantly enhanced. If, instead, the animal can sense and interpret a distant stimulus, such as the hawk's shadow, as a 'sign' for a hawk, then the animal can take timely evasive action. But this requires an ability to associate a (delayed) internal representation of the 'sign' (the shadow) with an abstracted or stored memory of a representation of the 'signified' (the hawk). And now we're really talking mind.

According to Humphrey, the evolution of consciousness involved the emergence of two distinct but complementary modes of representation: (1) internal representations of 'what is happening to me', that is the 'qualia of subjective feelings and first-person knowledge of the self', and (2) representations of 'what is happening out there,' of third-person 'intentional objects of cognition and objective knowledge of the external physical world' (1992, p. 44).

Sensation and Perception

We now come to the second major element of Humphrey's theory. Having established that the evolution of sensation may be explained as a natural consequence of increasing selectivity and sensitivity of the membrane encapsulating the individual organism, Humphrey's next step is to explain perception, and to emphasize how sensation and perception are different phenomena. His theory depends on interpreting sensation as oriented toward internal representations of 'what is happening to me' (subjective events), while perception is directed toward 'what is happening out there' (objective events). In other words, evolution has given organisms two distinct but complementary modes of experiencing the world, two 'alternative and essentially non-overlapping ways of interpreting the meaning of an environmental stimulus arriving at the body' (1992, p. 47).

He finds that this portion of his theory has antecedents among psychologists such as Freud and an 'obscure' psychologist of religion Edwin D. Starbuck, as well as in the writings of the eighteenth-century Scottish philosopher Thomas Reid (1710–1796). He quotes Reid from his *Essays on the Intellectual Powers of Man* (1785):

> The external senses have a double province — to make us feel, and to make us perceive. They furnish us with a variety of sensations, some pleasant, others painful, and others indifferent; at the same time they give us a conception of and an invincible belief in the existence of external objects. . . . This conception and belief which nature produces by means of the senses, we call *perception*. The feeling which goes along with perception, we call *sensation* (in Humphrey, 1992, p. 46).

Following Reid, Humphrey places great importance on the distinction between sensation and perception: *sensation* is 'what is happening to me' at *my* boundary. It involves an internal representation, or 'copy', of the stimulus as it concerns *this* membrane-encapsulated individual, this 'self' or 'ego'. The sensation carries with it an affect-quality: the stimulus is either 'good' or 'bad' (or neutral) for the 'self'. Sensation is immediately *felt* in the present; it is oriented toward subjective experience, related to 'I' or ego.

Perception, on the other hand, is about 'what is happening out there' beyond my boundary. It is about the external, objective world of events. Perception involves representations of 'signs' that signify something non-local; it is an *interpretation* about what the stimulus signifies about the state of the outside world. Since it is externally focused, perception is not about any specific 'ego/self' — that is, anyone can perceive the same object (whereas only '*I*' have the sensation of what is happening to me).

In a nutshell, then: *sensation* is an internal (subjective) *copy* of the stimulus; *perception* is an interpretation, a *story*, about (objective) significance in the outside world. For example, sensation is *feeling* the hawk's claws in my skin *now*; perception is seeing the shadow (or hearing the squawk) and inferring that there is a hawk close by — and if I don't do something in the very near *future* I will feel those razor-sharp talons.

The Basis of Consciousness

About halfway through the book, Humphrey begins to home in on his quarry. He has the silvery outline of the fish clearly in view, just below the surface. His hand is cupped underneath its belly, the tips of his fingers gently soothing its scales. He just needs to make a few more careful, charming moves before he scoops it out and lands it at his feet. One of the most important — and slippery — moves is to firmly establish sensation (as he has defined it) as the basis of consciousness. He lists eight assertions he believes he has already established:

(1) To be conscious is essentially to have sensations: that is, to have affect-laden mental representations of something happening here and now to me.
(2) The subject of consciousness, 'I', is an embodied self. In the absence of bodily sensations 'I' would cease. *Sentio, ergo sum* — I feel, therefore I am.
(3) All sensations are implicitly located at the spatial boundary between me and not-me, and at the temporal boundary between past and future: that is, the 'present'.
(5) Mental activities other than those involving direct sensations enter consciousness only insofar as they are accompanied by 'reminders' of sensation, such as happens in the case of mental imagery and dreams.
(6) If and when we claim that another living organism is conscious we are implying that it, too, is the subject of sensations (although not necessarily of a kind we are familiar with).
(7) If we were to claim that a non-living organism [such as a robot] was conscious, the same would have to apply (1992, pp. 115–6).

He then offers a more succinct definition of consciousness: 'to be conscious' is indeed essentially 'to have sensations' — or more generally 'to have affect-laden mental representations of something happening here and now to me' (1992, p. 120). And 'any theory of consciousness that is not a theory of the having of sensations has failed to address the *real problem*' — which is that consciousness 'has to involve the raw feel of "what it is like to be me"' (1992, p. 128).

Having committed himself to the virtual identity of sensation and consciousness, he goes on to reveal an apparent contradiction: 'namely that certain states of mind can also enter consciousness that do not arise directly from stimulation of the sense organs' (1992, p. 128). In order to resolve the 'contradiction', he says we have to answer the question 'What is it to have sensations?' And he re-emphasizes that 'the function of sensations is to provide the subject with representations of "what is happening to me" — originally to serve as a mediator of affect, but later with important secondary uses in connection with perception and imagery' (1992, pp. 129–30).

But he does more than merely repeat himself. Given the central importance of sensation in his argument, he devotes an entire chapter to the 'five characteristics' of sensation: 'sensations *characteristically* (1) belong to the subject, (2) are tied to a particular site in the body, (3) are present tense, (4) are modality-specific, (5) are self-characterizing in all these respects. In the *JCS* paper he lists these five 'defining properties of the experience of sensation' as 'ownership', 'bodily location', 'qualitative modality', 'presentness', and 'self-disclosing phenomenal immediacy'. We can now look at these individually.

(1) **Ownership**. *Sensation always belongs to the subject.* That is, 'what is happening to me' means what is happening to 'my *embodied* self', to that being inside the physical boundary between 'me' and 'not-me'. Only 'I' have my sensations — I *own* them, they are exclusively *mine*. No other bounded being has this relationship or point of view with regard to the sensations at this 'me/not-me' boundary. My first-person point of view is, thus, wholly dependent on the location of my own bounded body. I can, of course, have a third-person view of my own body, too; a view that can be shared by many other observers. In other words, I can also *perceive* my body, just as other people can. But only I can both perceive and sense what is happening to my body.

(2) **Bodily location**. *Sensation is always indexical and invokes a particular part of the subject's body.* This point has already been touched on above: namely that sensations always occur at some particular location, a location defined by the coordinates of the target body. Quite simply, I *always* feel a sensation at a *particular location* in or on my body (for example, if I taste something, it is associated with my mouth; if I feel something with my fingers, it is associated with my hand, and so on with the other senses). By contrast, my perceptions don't have to refer to any particular region of my body. I can perceive an object outside my body with any one or combination of my senses.

(3) **Presentness**. *Sensation is always present tense.* Whatever I sense is happening to me *always* happens in the present. 'Sensation is always *present tense, ongoing and imperfect*' (Humphrey, 2000, p. 14). 'That is to say every sensation persists for roughly so long as the surface stimulation continues' (1992, p. 137). Perceptions, on the other hand, can refer both to the past and future, as well as to the present. 'Perceptions unlike sensations do not *exist* for any length of time. . . . Perception itself is not an enduring entity with a life of its own . . . [it is] already complete — whereas sensations are generally . . . continuing and unfinished' (1992, p. 138).

(4) **Qualitative modality**. *Sensation always has the feel of several* qualitatively distinct modalities. All sensations belong to a distinctive sensory modality — vision, touch, hearing, smell, taste. 'Their absolute distinctiveness — the gulf between one modality and another — is one of the most mysterious facts about sensations. . . . There is no imaginable bridge' (1992, p. 136).[4] Perceptions, however, are never concerned with the nature of the stimulus as such, but with what it signifies about some condition in the external world.

(5) **Phenomenal immediacy**. '*Sensations tell their own story*' (1992, p. 138) Unlike perceptions which require interpretation, sensations are known directly and

---

[4] This seems to ignore the well-documented phenomenon of synaesthesia, where the usually clear distinction between the senses is bypassed or transcended. Some people can 'taste shapes', 'see sounds' or 'hear colors'. See, for instance, Richard Cytowic's *The Man Who Tasted Shapes* (1993).

immediately; they do not need to be inferred. 'Most important, sensation is always *phenomenally immediate*, and the four properties above are *self-disclosing*' (2000, p. 14).

Sensations are 'Instructions'

The next move, following elucidation of the five characteristics of sensations, is to explore more closely what is meant by the notion that 'I own my sensations', that they belong exclusively to me. (This move is not made in the *JCS* paper, but is key because it is the sense of exclusive ownership that gives rise to the distinction between subjectivity and objectivity.) Another term for 'exclusive' ownership is 'private' ownership. No one else has access to my sensations. No one else *ever* has access to *my* pain. By contrast, my perceptions are not exclusive or private: They belong in the public domain. They are objective. Any number of people can perceive the nail sticking into my toe — but only I *feel* it.

I own my sensations, therefore, in a way that I don't 'own' my perceptions. And it is this quality of ownership that is a major clue to Humphrey in his search for consciousness. In *History*, he spends a chapter or two investigating the concept of ownership and its relationship to 'volition'. He shows us how the notion of ownership is ultimately derived from our awareness of voluntary control over our own bodies. I know that this is *my* body ultimately by the test of whether or not it or its parts move when I will them to. That's the basic criterion for deciding between my body and what is not my body. From this, he goes on to ask whether ownership of sensations, likewise, is because — 'in some peculiar way' — they, too, are under executive orders? Answering this question affirmatively — that sensations are volitional or *intentional* (he coins the term 'sentition') — Humphrey wriggles his index finger and tickles the fish a little bit more. He's pointing at a line of argument that concludes:

> [Any] mental state will be self-indicating if and only if it both refers to a particular site in the body and produces a physical disturbance at the very site referred to. . . . In fact any mental state that unites these two elements of referring to a site in the body and reaching out to create a disturbance at this site would belong to the class of bodily activities by definition. . . . We can conclude that sensations themselves are indeed a form of bodily activity (1992, pp. 155–6).

Sensations, in other words, are *instructions*. They are issued by the bounded self (in the form of nerve signals), directed to a particular site on its body to *create a physical disturbance at that particular bodily location*. Contrary to what people usually believe: Sensations don't just *happen to* us; they happen because we *create* them in response to a stimulus.

> Being 'sensitive' need have meant, to begin with, nothing more complicated than being locally reactive: in other words, responding selectively at the place where the surface stimulus occurred (1992, p. 157).

Later on in evolution, when organisms developed nervous systems, they began relaying information from one part of the skin to other parts and caused reactions there; and those *self-initiated* reactions were felt as sensations at those other locations. The relayed and delayed reactions resulted in flexible patterns of action that *represented* the original stimulus. These 'action patterns' were *affective*, in that they discriminated between welcome and unwelcome stimuli. Humphrey moves in closer now: '. . . sensitivity evolved primarily as a means of *doing something about the stimulus at the point of stimulation* . . .' (1992).

The activity of sensing, even in human beings, is a direct descendent of the primitive affective response. The 'sensory loop' has gradually lengthened. Nevertheless an unbroken tradition links the sensations of modern human beings to those original amoeboid wriggles of acceptance or rejection (1992, p. 159).

Humphrey is moving, deliberately and carefully, toward the conclusion that what began in evolution as a local surface response to an external stimulus later became a centralized representation of a flexible action pattern (or set of instructions). In other words, what began as a real *bodily* activity, evolved into some sort of *brain* activity: 'Sensations involve a sensory response, with a signal being sent from a central site back out to a peripheral location (originally to the body surface itself but later to a surrogate location at the cortex of the brain)' (1992, p. 179).

The 'Thick Moment' of the Extended Present

The physicalist core of Humphrey's theory of consciousness — and where it differs ontologically from panexperientialist and idealist theories — is the derivation of sensation from mechanical reactivity at the boundary or surface of a membrane-encapsulated 'packet of worldstuff' — wholly insensate worldstuff, at that. Sensation, then, is ultimately nothing more than highly refined loops of mechanical reactions of otherwise inert matter. And since, as we have seen, he defines consciousness in terms of sensation, he effectively presents a mechanical, materialist explanation of consciousness.[5] Mind equals brain.

His challenge is to make his explanation account for the peculiar characteristics of consciousness, such as its 'raw feel', its subjectivity, its qualia, its first-person perspective, its in-the-present quality, its intentionality and meaningfulness. And he claims to have done just this by describing the evolution of sensation from primitive acceptance–rejection responses to sophisticated representations of flexible action patterns centrally located in the brain. A critical element in the development of this theory is the argument that *sensations are intentional* — that sensations are created by the host organism in the form of 'instructions' relayed from the central nervous system to the periphery where they *create a physical disturbance*. This 'physical disturbance' is what the organism experiences as the sensation.

However, there is a problem: If all the organism has to work with is 'insensate raw stuff', purely physical matter, how could it produce *instructions*? It could certainly send 'signals' down the nerve fibres (computers do something similar all the time), but signals differ from instructions in one critical respect. Whereas signals convey information from one location to another, 'instructions' also involve intentionality and *anticipation*. Instructions convey an intended effect yet to be realized. In other words, instructions are oriented toward the future. This is a real problem for a physicalist theory of brain–mind relations. And it's a problem that Humphrey

---

[5] Incidentally, it may be that only a materialist *could* offer an explanation of consciousness. Since all the other ontologies — dualism, panexperientialism, idealism — *begin* with consciousness or experience as a metaphysical given, it is beyond explanation. From the viewpoint of these ontologies, it would be as meaningful to attempt to *explain* consciousness (in the sense of providing a causal theory) as to attempt to explain being, or existence. Since materialists start with the assumption of pure matter, they are required to account for consciousness via an explanation of how it emerged. However, the situation is very different when we come to consider the relationship between consciousness and matter. Here *all* ontologies are required to present an explanation.

recognized: 'No signal, no matter what its *effects* are, can be an instruction unless its sender *already has these effects in mind*' (1992, p. 181).

One reason this is a major problem is that it threatens to send the theory off into an infinite regress. For the whole point of the theory is to provide an *explanation* of consciousness, yet here we seem to be compelled to assume that key elements of the theory themselves *already* possess mind or consciousness — namely, the brain cells involved in sending the instructions down the nerve fibres. And if the brain cells are conscious experiencing entities, how do we explain *that*? If their molecules are conscious . . . etc. The 'infinite regress', of course, is panexperientialism — consciousness all the way down.

Since Humphrey is decidedly not out to present a panexperientialist theory, he is committed to avoiding the infinite regress of mind at all costs. And, consistent with the ingenuity of his theory so far, he comes up with a novel solution — the hypothesis of the 'extended present' or the 'thick moment of consciousness'; a solution on which his theory of physicalist mind–brain identity is precariously balanced:

> For I believe that ultimately the key to an experience being 'like something' does in fact lie in the experience *being like itself in time* — hence *being about itself*, or *taking itself as its own intentional object*. And this is achieved, in the special case of sensory responses, through a kind of *self-resonance* that effectively stretches out the present moment to create what I have called the *thick moment of consciousness* (Humphrey, 2000, p. 15).

And it may be just at this point where we discover his theory's Achilles' heel. I will come back to this shortly, but for now it's interesting to note that his theory is potentially vulnerable just at the point where panexperientialism threatens to come back into the story.

Admitting that 'a signal, just on its own, *cannot* amount to an instruction' and that a 'pattern of nerve impulses travelling either to the body surface or the cortex cannot just on its own constitute an instruction' (1992, p. 181), Humphrey's creative leap is to stretch time and insert a feedback loop. A 'signal' can become an 'instruction', he proposes, if a return signal from the body's surface informs the brain of the fate of the original signal. Thus, once in possession of the 'end-state' information, the brain would 'know' what the effect would be and therefore could anticipate the result. Such a scenario would, of course, involve 'backward causation in time', where a future event informs or changes the state of a prior event. And *this* blatantly contradicts one of the foundation principles of physicalist science: the law of causality. This law states that a cause must necessarily (and therefore *always*) precede its effect. In fact, this is how 'cause' and 'effect' are defined, in terms of their sequential, temporal relations.

So Humphrey, in his efforts to provide a logical, coherent, and comprehensive explanation for the evolution of consciousness from wholly insensate matter, now finds himself on shaky ground. He is in real danger of slipping into the stream and scaring off the fish once and for all. His physicalist theory has come to this: In order to take the next step he is compelled to violate the very foundation of the system of physics he draws on to support his theory. He is about to fall into a fatal *reductio ad absurdum*.

But he recovers his equilibrium enough to make his decisive move: Admitting that 'What becomes of something in the *future* . . . cannot change its *present* meaning', he counters that it all depends on what is meant by 'present meaning': in particular, on when the 'present' happens and on how long the 'present' lasts. Suppose the present were to be stretched out a bit. Suppose it were to last long enough for the present and the past to overlap (1992, p. 183).

In other words, what if the present moment was stretched sufficiently for the outgoing and return signals to overlap or interleaf their information. In such a situation, the outgoing signal could 'know' what happened at the 'end' of the line *before the outgoing signal completed its journey*. Now in possession of the 'end-state' information, the original signal could anticipate its own effect and thereby qualify as an 'instruction.' Et voila! Humphrey weaves in the problematic anticipatory and intentional qualities of instructions into a purely physical system of feedback loops. He has turned water into wine, and landed the fish in the frying pan in one fell swoop.

> Conscious feeling, it has emerged, is a remarkable kind of intentional doing. Feelings enter consciousness, not as events that happen *to us* but as *activities* that we ourselves engender and participate in — activities that loop back on themselves to create the thick moment of the subjective present. . . . All we seem to have ended up with is a string of nerve impulses, or information, flowing around a physical circuit in the brain (Humphrey, 1992, p. 217).

But not so fast. Let's run that story by one more time. As Humphrey says, it all depends on what we mean by the 'present', and 'how long the present lasts'. It all depends, in other words, on stretching time; by replacing the notion of instantaneous present with the notion of 'extended present' or the 'thickened moment'. But how, exactly, does this feat come about? Is it any easier, or more meaningful, to 'stretch the present', than to turn water into wine? In physics, the present has even less duration than a quantum has space. In fact, the present has no duration, or at best an infinitely short duration (which amounts to the same thing). Humphrey's final solution is to bifurcate time into what he calls 'physical present' and 'subjective present'.

> The 'physical present', strictly speaking, is a mathematical abstraction of infinitely short duration, and nothing happens in it. By contrast the 'subjective present' is arguably the carrier and *container* of our conscious life, and everything that ever happens to us happens *in it* (1992, p. 183).

But where did the 'subjective present' come from? It can't have come from the feedback loop of brain-sensation signals, since that is precisely what was *required* to allow the feedback loop to turn signals into instructions in the first place. It showed up in the theory as an *ad hoc* insertion by Humphrey *because his own theory compelled him to do so*. The theory contains *no explanation* for the appearance of 'subjective time'.

In order to avoid the infinite regress of panexperientialism, Humphrey had to bifurcate time, and invoke the ghost of subjectivity out of thin air (you can't have 'subjective time' without subjectivity). Or, rather, he invoked subjectivity out of the raw material of his feedback loops. Either he created subjectivity out of nothing, or it was there *all the time* in the 'packets of worldstuff' from which the feedback loops evolved. Since it makes no sense to say he created subjectivity out of nothing, we must conclude that it was there all along, intrinsic to the raw material of evolution.

The problem with Humphrey's theory is not so much the idea of 'subjective time' as contrasted with 'physical time'. After all, as he said, the physicist's time is merely a mathematical abstraction of infinitesimal duration, or, alternatively, the physicist's time is reduced to a dimension of space, completely devoid of any durational or experiential qualities. Rather than being problematical, then, subjective time may well be the only meaningful way of understanding durational time. Panexperientialists, such as David Griffin (1986), would be sympathetic to Humphrey's need to introduce the 'subjective present', and would agree with his statement that the '"subjective present" is arguably the carrier and *container* of our conscious life, and everything that ever happens to us happens *in it*' — because, they would say, that's the only kind of present there is.

Ironically, then, Humphrey's theory stands or falls on the notion of 'subjective present', and if it stands, it does so because it must accept the panexperientialist ontology that subjectivity was present in matter all down the line. It was there in the first wiggles of the first amoebae, in the molecules that filtered through its boundary wall, and in the molecules of the membrane itself; it was there in the first self-replicating molecules, and in the atoms that constituted their helical spines; it was there in the primeval chemical soup, and in the photons radiating down on them from a sun more than ninety million miles away; it was there in the nuclear reactions in the hearts of the stars themselves; and it was there in the primordial plasma-radiation that filled the universe in the first few moments after the Big Bang. And it was there, too.

Despite Humphrey's clever and coherent analysis of the origins and evolution of sensations and consciousness, an analysis rich in subtleties and hues of logic and experimental data, he still ends up with coloured water, thinking he has produced the 'wine of consciousness'. His coloured water is a very good facsimile of the best vintage — but it is still only 'fools wine'. Despite the almost imperceptible sleight of hand by which he introduced the 'dye' of the subjective present, his physical facsimile of consciousness cannot produce the miracle. The fish is off the hook.

In the end — as with all physicalist theories of consciousness — no amount or complexity of feedback and/or feedforward loops of insentient, non-subjective 'worldstuff' can ever make the ontological leap and produce the 'wine-from-water' miracle of subjective experience. Even inspired by the genius of his hero Thomas Reid, Humphrey's mind–brain equation *(m = b)* does not balance out. The left-hand 'm' (tingling with veridical subjectivity) cannot be the same 'kind' as the right-hand 'b' (if it's ultimately made up of wholly non-subjective matter). Given the foundational premise of insentient matter–energy at the base of materialism, and despite a valiant attempt to bridge the ontological gap, Humphrey ends up falling victim to the ontological fallacy that consciousness is physical, that subjectivity even *could be* objective matter complexified. 'Mark Twain cannot equal Midsummer Day'. The inconceivable remains inconceivable.

References

Cytowic, R.E. (1993), *The Man Who Tasted Shapes* (New York: Tarcher/Putnam).
de Quincey, C. (1994), 'Consciousness all the way down? An analysis of McGinn's critique of panexperientialism', *Journal of Consciousness Studies*, **1** (2), pp. 217–29.
de Quincey, C. (1999), 'Past matter, present mind: A convergence of worldviews', *JCS*, **6** (1), pp. 91–106.
Griffin, D R. (ed. 1986), *Physics and the Ultimate Significance of Time* (Albany: SUNY).
Humphrey, N. (1992), *A history of the mind* (New York: Simon & Schuster).
Humphrey, N. (1995), 'The thick moment', in *The Third Culture: Beyond the Scientific Revolution*, ed. J. Brockman (New York: Simon & Schuster).
Humphrey, N. (2000), 'How to solve the mind–body problem', *JCS*, **7** (4), pp. 5–20 (this issue).
McGinn, C. (1991), *The Problem of Consciousness: Toward a Solution* (Oxford: Blackwell).
Nagel, T. (1986), *The View From Nowhere* (Oxford: Oxford University Press).

Carol Rovane

Not Mind–Body but Mind–Mind

My comment will focus on the following five claims of Humphrey's. At some points I will be drawing on his book *A History of the Mind* as well as the target article in this issue.

(1) The qualitative aspects of phenomenal consciousness belong exclusively to sensation.

(2) The qualitative aspects of sensation are adequately characterized in terms of five properties: they are owned; they have a bodily location; they occur in the temporal present; they come in a sensory modality; they disclose all this about themselves.

(3) This characterization of sensation in terms of these five properties does better justice to what sensations are like than the standard functionalist accounts.

(4) All five of the properties and, hence, the qualitative aspects of sensation can be accounted for as arising from a certain structure of stimulation and response.

(5) This account affords real progress on the mind–body problem because the structure that, according to it, gives rise to the qualitative aspects of sensation can coherently be attributed to neural processes in the brain.

(1) According to Humphrey, sensations — in the sense that involves one or other sensory modality (in the human case, eyesight, hearing, touch, smell or taste) — are the sole contributors of qualitative feeling to mental life. So, if it ever seems as though there is something it is like to be in a mental state of another kind, such as perceiving or believing or wanting or intending, it is only because that state somehow involves or is accompanied by sensation.

When Humphrey confines the qualitative aspects of consciousness to sensation, he parts company with William James, who famously held that each item in the stream of consciousness has its own distinctive feel, including even an 'and' feeling, an 'if' feeling and a 'but' feeling. He also parts company with many contemporary philosophers of mind, such as Nagel and Searle, who affirm that it is in the nature of *any* mental state that it is the sort of thing that *can* appear in consciousness. It would not be enough for them that a subject have what Humphrey is willing to grant here, namely, 'access consciousness' to the state. In addition, there must be *something it is like* for the subject to be in that state — what Humphrey calls 'phenomenal consciousness'.

Oddly enough, I have not yet figured out where I stand on this dispute between the more generous views of phenomenal consciousness and Humphrey's narrower,

Journal of Consciousness Studies, **7**, No. 4, 2000, pp. 82–92

sensationalist, view of it. This shows that I do not regard myself as a complete authority over the contents of my own consciousness. Yet I know that others do so regard themselves. And this makes me wonder how disputes about the extent of phenomenal consciousness could ever be satisfactorily resolved. In particular, I can't imagine how Humphrey could ever convince James that he was wrong about there being a 'but' feeling, or Nagel that he is wrong about there being something it is like to believe in democracy. After all, only James and Nagel — not Humphrey — can pronounce authoritatively on what does or does not appear to them phenomenally. From where I write this comment (Hyderabad), I do not have access to enough of Humphrey's published writings to assure myself that I understand exactly why he feels free to disregard such pronouncements of others. What I can do, though, is show how his account of phenomenal consciousness can be extended so as to cover alleged non-sensory cases as well. But that must wait until the end, after I have considered the account on its own terms.

In the meantime, I want to make clear that the interest of Humphrey's account of phenomenal consciousness does not hinge on his being right to take the narrow sensationalist view of it, and this is so even if I am wrong about the extendibility of the account to alleged non-sensory cases. It would be a major contribution to just to have accounted for the sensory case alone, even if other cases remain to be accounted for.

(2) As for the adequacy of Humphrey's characterization of sensation, I don't really see what more would be required in order that there be something it is like to have sensations than that they have the five properties in terms of which he characterizes them — that is, that they are owned, in a bodily location, in the temporal present, in a sensory modality and, moreover, disclose all this about themselves. I would add only a minor qualification which, I think, he intends anyway. The qualification is that these properties be understood as having the requisite specificity. For example, when I tasted papaya this morning, my sensation disclosed itself not merely as *owned* but as *mine*; not merely as *having a bodily location* but as *in my mouth*; not merely as *in the temporal present* but as *happening at the particular time it did* (specified in a way adequate to context — in this case, breakfast time today); not merely as *in a sensory modality* but as *a taste* and, moreover, as *tasting the way it does* (i.e., like papaya, not quinine).

(3) One trouble with functionalism, at least in the eyes of many, is that it hasn't afforded a satisfactory account of the specifically qualitative aspects of sensation. Speaking very generally and roughly, there are two main strategies of functional reduction. One assimilates qualia to perception — thus what it is like to see a red rose or smell it is just to know through one's eyes that it is red or to know through one's nose that it is sweet (this is sometimes portrayed as a kind of knowing how). The other links qualia to a higher order capacity to self-ascribe or avow mental states — thus what it's like to feel pain is afforded not merely by the fact that one is in a state with the characteristic functional role of pain, but by the additional fact that one is able to self-ascribe and/or avow the state.

If it is a mistake for functionalists to try to reduce qualia to perception, then Humphrey's account has at least the minimal advantage of not making that mistake. Following Thomas Reid, he argues that sensation has a very different function from perception. Whereas the function of perception is to represent states of affairs in the external world, the function of sensation is to monitor internal somatic conditions. It should be obvious that this separation of function is consistent with there being a fairly systematic connection as well. After all, somatic conditions tend to reflect environmental conditions and, so, the sensations that monitor somatic conditions will typically provide information which is relevant to the representational task of perception. But although Humphrey thus provides for a systematic connection between sensation and perception, he also emphasizes that they can come apart. On the basis of his research on blindsight, he argues that it is possible to see — i.e. to perceive with one's eyes — without having any accompanying visual sensations and, hence, without there being anything that the seeing is like. He also claims that different sensory modalities can be the source of the same perceptually relevant information. Although this latter claim is not as controversial as his claim about blindsight, his way of defending it is nevertheless highly original. Rather than defending it in the usual way, by pointing to the fact that it is possible to perceive the same property (for example, a shape) through different sensory modalities (for example, through sight and touch), he offers a wonderfully imaginative discussion of what he calls 'skinvision'. This is a form of perception in which the sensory modality of touch not only provides perceptual knowledge of the same things we normally perceive through eyesight but, also, it does so in the same way — i.e. through the way that light affects us.

If it is a mistake for functionalists to try to reduce qualia to some kind of self-ascription (or the capacity for it), then Humphrey's account avoids also this mistake. Of course, his account does provide for a close connection between the qualitative aspects of phenomenal consciousness and the capacity to self-ascribe what one is conscious of. This is ensured by the first and last properties that he attributes to sensation — that they are owned and that they disclose themselves to us in this way, as being (among other things) owned. But he does not aim to capture what sensations are like just in terms of these two properties. He aims to do so by bringing in all five of the properties he attributes to them. So, in his view, what sensations are like consists in their disclosing themselves to us not only as owned but, also, as located in the body and as occurring in the temporal present and as coming in a sensory modality.

All things considered, I think we should grant that Humphrey has done better justice to the qualitative aspects of sensation than the standard functionalist alternatives. Though, again, I would add the qualification that the five properties in terms of which he characterizes what sensations are like be construed as having the requisite specificity.

(4) How, then, does Humphrey propose to account for the five properties in terms of which he characterizes what sensations are like? His pivotal idea is that sensations are *responses* to stimulations. He infers from this that they are a kind of *action*. And, he proposes to account for all five of the properties by showing how and why they figure as properties of action. Take the first property, of being owned by a subject. Echoing Locke on the connection between property and labour, he declares that ownership of anything (such as one's body) arises with intentional control over it. So the property of being owned is automatically provided for by the mere fact that sensations are actions. In (mild) contrast, the second property, bodily locatedness, is not automatically provided for by the mere fact that sensations are actions. It depends on the particular kind of action that sensations involve or, I should say, are. As I just explained, sensations are a kind of response to a stimulation. And, according to Humphrey, the particular kind of action that they are is one of 'reaching out' to the stimulation. The bodily locatedness of a sensation is due, therefore, to the bodily locatedness of the stimulation to which it reaches out. [NB I have omitted a detail which doesn't matter

here, but which will resurface later in my comment, which is that the bodily location of the stimulus–response pair is not literal but representational. The stimulation first makes its way inward from an initial point of entry at the body's surface to a corresponding location on a mental representation of the body. And the response to the stimulation reaches no further than this internal, representa- tional site. This detail enables Humphrey to explain the phantom limb phenomenon in which sensations are experienced as located in non-existent bodily parts.] I can't say I fully understand Humphrey's account of the third property, temporal presentness — though I find it fascinating. Again, he appeals to the particular kind of actions that he thinks sensations are. In his view, a sensation does not merely consist in a simple response of reaching out to a stimulation; in addition, the response generates a reverberant feedback loop in which both the stimulation and the response keep each other going for an interval of time. The property of occurring in the temporal present is supposed to arise somehow from the way in which such a feedback loop fills time. As for the property of sensory modality, that too has to do with the active nature of sensation. Just as there are different modes or ways in which we act with our bodies, so also there are different modes or ways in which we act internally in response to various kinds of stimulation. And finally, the fifth property, self-disclosure, is likewise a feature of action. Just as you can't act without knowing what you're up to, so also you can't have the sorts of responses that constitute sensations without knowing what you're up to. By Humphrey's lights, this means you know your sensations have the other four properties — they are yours, in a bodily location, in the temporal present and in a sensory modality. So when he says that sensations have the property of being self-disclosing, he is really saying that each of the other four properties of sensations is itself self-disclosing. As with the property of temporal presentness, I can't say I fully understand everything he has to say about self-disclosure. He sees both properties as arising somehow from the nature of the feedback loops that sensations involve. As these loops reverberate and fill time they also take on the character of being 'self-representing': they become 'signals of themselves'. It should be obvious that this character is a necessary condition for the property of being self-disclosing (indeed, the character and the property may even be identical). It may not be obvious that it is a necessary condition for having the property of temporal presentness as well. But it is. For, if a feedback loop lacked all such representational significance, it could only fill time *mutely* as it were; it could not become temporally present *to* a subject.

Before trying to evaluate this account of how the qualitative aspects of sensation arise, let me make a few background remarks about the way in which the account brings evolutionary considerations to bear. As far as Humphrey is concerned, it is a necessary condition on any adequate account of the qualitative aspects of sensation that it afford a plausible evolutionary story about them. His own story is as follows: sensations are originally descended from 'amoebic wriggles of acceptance or rejection' of items impinging at the body surface; these later evolved into internal 'affective responses of like and dislike'; sensations finally emerged when these responses came to have the five properties in terms of in which he characterizes their qualitative aspects. This story is intrinsically interesting. It has the added merit of lending further plausibility to Humphrey's pivotal idea recounted in the preceding paragraph, which is that sensations are a species of action. But, ultimately, I don't think the evolutionary details make any *direct* contribution to his account of the qualitative aspects of sensation. It is natural enough to suppose otherwise, as I myself did on a first reading of *A History of the Mind*. For, when Humphrey portrays sensations as descended from a species of affect-laden activity, he implicitly taps into our sense that there is something it is like to have affective responses and to act intentionally. And this might naturally lead one to suppose that he aims to account for what sensations are like in terms of what affect and action are like. But it should be clear to readers of this comment that this supposition reflects a misunderstanding of Humphrey's project. Per claim (1), he holds that sensations are the sole contributors of felt quality to mental life. And, so, he cannot possibly propose to account for their felt quality in this way, by appealing to our implicit sense that there is something it is like to have affective responses and to act intentionally. He can appeal only to the structure of stimulation and response which, in his account, gives rise to the five properties that belong exclusively to sensations and that constitute the felt quality that they exclusively have.

So let's see how the account works through an example. Take again the taste of papaya that I experienced this morning. According to the account, I was first stimulated at my body surface by papaya against my tongue. The stimulation then travelled inwards to a mental representation of my body and landed at the representational site of my tongue. I responded by reaching out to the stimulation at that site in a way that generated a feedback loop (my reaching out to the stimulation kept it alive long enough to stimulate another reaching out to it, and so on until the process petered out). In reaching out to the stimulation, I registered the following: that the reaching out was mine; that it was a reaching out to the tongue region; that it was filling up the temporal present (which was then breakfast time); that it involved tasting rather than, say, touching and, furthermore, tasting in the papaya way rather than some other way (such as the quinine way). Insofar as I registered all of these properties, they qualify as having been self-disclosing. And that takes care of all five of the properties in terms of which Humphrey characterizes what sensations are like — though I have taken the liberty of describing the properties at the level of specificity that I think is required in order to adequately capture what my sensation was like.

So far so good. But where, in this account, was the felt quality of my sensation? I said above that Humphrey portrays it as involving all five properties. But when I reflect on what it was like, the two properties that stand out most vividly are its locatedness and its modality. Again, I am thinking of these properties with the requisite specificity: what stood out about my sensation was its being at my tongue with the papaya taste. And how, exactly, was that accounted for? By the particular way in which I reached out to the stimulation that was initiated by the papaya against my tongue. Humphrey's claim is that I reached out to my tongue representation in the tasting way, and I would qualify that as the papaya-tasting way. But this claim leaves us with the following crucial question: *what is it about the papaya-tasting way of reaching out to a stimulation that ensures that there is something it is like to do it*? In other words, why can't such a reaching out resemble blindsight as he characterizes that phenomenon, which is to say, why can't it be a blind process in which cognitive and other functional work gets done without any qualitative accompaniment? I don't think Humphrey has (yet) provided a fully satisfactory answer to this question.

In raising the question, I am raising the sort of objection that Kripke raised against all forms of materialism, including functionalism. It might seem premature that the objection should come up now, since the mind–body problem isn't actually under discussion yet — that comes under the heading of claim (5). But the objection has an extremely general thrust, which is that the qualitative aspects of mental life simply cannot be accounted for in purely structural terms. This is supposed to be so regardless of whether they are the terms of neurophysiology or the standard functionalist accounts or, I'll now add, Humphrey's reverberant feedback loops. For the objection says that *any* such structure is imaginable without there being anything it is like.

I am not raising this objection because I think Humphrey should be deterred by it. I'll explain why I don't think he should be deterred by it below, after a very brief discussion of his fifth claim.

(5) If Humphrey's fourth claim were irreproachable — that is, if there could be no challenge to his claim to have adequately accounted for the qualitative aspects of sensation in purely structural terms — then he could truly be said to have made progress on the mind–body problem. He is absolutely right that the structure in question, of stimulation and response giving rise to feedback loops and so on, can coherently be attributed to neural processes in the brain. However, as I just explained above, the difficulty is that Kripke-style considerations can be used to challenge his fourth claim.

Back to (4). On what grounds, then, might Humphrey set the Kripke-style objection aside? First option. Many materialists and functionalists have argued that if qualia are deprived of all material nature and functional role, then they must be merely epiphenomenal. Humphrey could follow suit, and insist that any qualitative aspect of sensation that is not accounted for by his structure must be merely epiphenomenal. Clearly, this response would not be in keeping with the spirit of his project. He does not want to make the mind–body problem easy by relegating qualia to the status of mere epiphenomena. He wants first to make the problem hard by doing full justice to the qualitative aspects of sensation, and then to show that the problem can nevertheless be solved.

Second option. He could echo various optimistic materialists who insist that the more structural affinities and isomorphisms we find between mind and body, the less we will be struck or moved by Kripke-style considerations. If these optimistic materialists are right, then the mind–body problem is not a philosophical problem but an empirical one. I suspect that these philosophers are right and that Humphrey would agree. But all the same, I don't think he — or we — should harbour any illusions about having satisfied those philosophers who are moved by Kripke-style considerations. They believe that they know *a priori* that no structure of the sort he has posited could fully account for the qualitative aspects of sensation. The reason why is that they can imagine all such structures without any qualitative accompaniments. And no materialist, including Humphrey, has yet proven to their satisfaction that what they find it so easy to imagine is not really possible.

Third option. He could set the mind–body problem aside on the ground that we won't be ready to tackle it until we have solved a prior problem that I'll call the 'mind–mind' problem. This is the problem we should throw back in the face of those philosophers who claim, on the basis of Kripke-style considerations, that the mind–body problem is insoluble. It concerns how the qualitative aspects of mental life relate not to *body*, but to other aspects of *mental* life, such as intentionality, rationality, motivation and action. At present, we don't really know whether it is the case or, if so, why it should be the case that the former are a necessary condition for the latter. And, because we don't know this, we are precipitate whenever we try to make

pronouncements about the mind–body relation — regardless of whether our pronouncements are in favour of dualism, epiphenomenalism, materialism or functionalism. In fact, I would go so far as to say that all philosophers who make confident
pronouncements about the mind–body relation are really just manifesting, in one way
or another, their ignorance about the mind–mind relation. For consider. Why are pro-
ponents of the Kripke-style objection so confident that they can imagine that a given
material system might be able to perform various cognitive and practical tasks even
though there is nothing it is like for the system to do so? It's because we have so little
idea about what role qualia play in those tasks. The very same ignorance is what
makes the first option of response to Kripke — the counter-charge that qualia must be
merely epiphenomenal — so tempting. It is indeed tempting to think of them as
epiphenomenal when we have so little positive idea about what contribution they
make to mental life. For the very same reason, it is also understandable that propo-
nents of the Kripke-style objection remain unconvinced by the various reductive proposals that have been put forward by optimistic materialists and functionalists. Given
our present state of understanding, such proposals are only so much hand waving. Of
course, as I've already conceded, those who are moved by Kripke-style considerations think things are worse than that for the optimistic materialists, because they
think they know *a priori* that qualia are irreducible to any material or functional
terms. But they are no more able to convince the materialists and functionalists than
the materialists and functionalists are able to convince them; nor are they able to say
why the qualitative residue that they say is bound to resist all material and functional
characterization is not, as some have charged in response to them, merely
epiphenomenal. The reason why is again the same: they have nothing positive to say
about what role qualia play in mental life. All they offer is a blanket conviction that it
is an *essential* feature of mindedness in general — if not of every mental particular —
that there be something it is like. But it is not at all clear why we should retain this
conviction in the light of their own arguments. For what they have shown is that a
great many other aspects of mind, such as the ability to use language and solve problems and so on, are imaginable without any qualitative accompaniment. My point is
not that we should therefore conclude that Kripke *et al*. are wrong about the
essentialness of qualia to mindedness. Nor is my point that we should conclude that
qualia are epiphenomenal. My point is that *none* of the main parties to the current dispute about the relation to mind and body — not the essentialists who oppose reduction nor the optimistic materialists who attempt reduction nor the more cautious
optimists who claim that any unreduced qualitative remainder must be merely
epiphenomenal — can be said to have clearly won out over the others. And the reason
why is in every case the same, namely, our current ignorance about the relation of
qualia to other aspects of mind. So, in my view, anyone who has anything illuminat-
ing to say about the 'mind–mind' relation is perfectly justified in proceeding even if
they don't (yet) have a 'shut-up' response to the Kripke-style objection. And
Humphrey is in this happy position. Indeed, it is striking how much of his account of
the qualitative aspects of sensation is devoted to situating them in relation to other
mental phenomena, especially perception, affect and action. And I recommend that
he continue in this vein, and leave the mind–body problem to sort itself out later.

Let me briefly try to say what progress I think Humphrey has already afforded on
the mind–mind problem. One of the main virtues of his approach is that it leaves

behind philosophical preoccupations with the issue of essentialism, substituting instead issues that are empirically tractable — if not by controlled experiment, then at least by appeal to evolutionary considerations.

Now, it does seem to me (and many others) that what sensations are like does not play any *essential* role in their contributions to perception and other cognitive functions. Philosophers typically confirm this point by *a priori* reflection on such possibilities as inverted spectra and absent qualia — often with the result that they worry whether the very idea of qualia might be vacuous or incoherent (a beetle in a box). In contrast, Humphrey confirms the same point with empirical work on blindsight and, also, empirically informed speculations about what 'skinvision' would be like — with the result that there is no worry at all about vacuousness or incoherence. Furthermore, he confirms this without compromising the fact that sensations do make a cognitive contribution to mental life as well as a 'felt' one. For, in his account, the cognitive contribution of sensations has more to do with their function, which is to monitor internal somatic conditions, than it has to do with the particular way in which they perform that function by generating the sorts of feedback loops that he claims give rise to their qualitative aspects.

It might seem more plausible that there is an essential connection between what sensations are like and their affective and motivational significance. But the only case about which there is any real consensus is pain, which we generally don't like and try to avoid. Otherwise, although it is a fact that we are generally affected and moved by the way sensations feel, it is hard to say why there should be any *essential* connection here. That is, it is hard to say why the particular ways that sensations feel to us – for example, the way colours look to us — should necessarily affect or move us in the ways they do. (I myself have often wondered about people who, unlike myself, hate to be tickled. Do they hate it because it feels different to them or do they just hate the way it feels? I can't say. And this means I can't say that there is an essential connection between the way it feels and liking or not liking it.) In Humphrey's account, the affective and motivational significance of sensations is guaranteed by their evolutionary origins in the somatic responses of primitive organisms ('amoebic wriggles of acceptance and rejection'). But this connection is not an essential one in the philosophers' sense; it is a connection made by historical accident. This helps to account for why it seems to us that the connection is real and important even though we can't, as philosophers, show it to be essential.

Similarly, Humphrey's evolutionary perspective also helps to explain away some of our philosophical perplexities about the connections — and/or lacks thereof — between sensation and perception. Looked at in one way, it is, of course, not accidental that sensations, qua events that monitor internal somatic conditions, should also monitor environmental conditions; for it is not accidental that somatic conditions reflect environmental conditions. But all the same, it is an evolutionary accident that the particular ways in which we perceive objects in our environments is bound up with the particular sensory capacities we happen to have — that we see things, for example, as well as touch them and that we see them with our eyes rather than with our skin.

In short, Humphrey's account of the position of qualia in mental life is the most promising and fertile I have seen. I am especially impressed by his pivotal idea that sensation is itself a species of affect-laden intentional activity. This is a genuinely new idea with enormous appeal and explanatory potential, the full measure of which I suspect not even he has taken. And I want to reiterate: the fact that he does not (yet) have a 'shut-up' response to the Kripke-style objection is no reason at all to abandon the idea.

Back to (1). Insofar as Humphrey aims to do full justice to the qualitative aspects of sensation in particular, it is fair enough that he should want to emphasize the ways in which sensations are unlike anything else we are acquainted with in mental life. As he puts it, they have a thickness and a resonance that is simply missing in other mental phenomena. He is surely right about this. But nonetheless, what I find most impressive and, indeed, powerful about his account of sensations is that it brings out how much they have in common with other mental phenomena, in particular with intentional action. It should not be surprising, therefore, that the account can be extended to other alleged cases of phenomenal consciousness besides the sensory case that he had in mind when he framed the account.

Let me take as an example of non-sensory phenomenal consciousness my current state of attending, which is an attending to the idea of a reverberant feedback loop. It does seem to me that there is something it is like to do this. Admittedly, there are sensory accompaniments of the sort that Humphrey likes to emphasize. I'm aware of visual and auditory aspects of images and words that come to mind as I think. But it also seems to me that I'm managing to hold the *idea itself* in my mind and, moreover, (I'm afraid I'm repeating myself) that there is something it is like to do this. Obviously, this conscious episode can't have all five of the properties in terms of which Humphrey characterizes what sensations are like. Being non-sensory, the episode is bound to lack the second property, bodily locatedness, and the fourth property, sensory modality. But it certainly has the other three: it is mine, it is in the present, and it discloses itself as the very state it is, namely, my present attending to the idea of a reverberant feedback loop. And I find it perfectly plausible that these three properties could fall out of the very sort of structure stimulation and response in terms of which Humphrey accounts for all five of the properties that he attributes to sensation — perhaps not the very *same* structure, but a very *similar* one. The stimulation would, of course, have to be different. It wouldn't originate at the body's surface as sensory stimulations do. It would have to be the deliverance of something like Locke's 'reflection' or Kant's 'inner sense' — the effect of an occurrence within the mind upon the mind itself. Once such an internal stimulation occurred there would have to be a response of 'reaching out' to it in more or less the way Humphrey describes in the case of sensation: the response would have to create a disturbance at the site of the stimulation, with the result that both the stimulation and the response generate a reverberant feedback loop in which they keep each other going for a while. Frankly, this is pretty much what attending feels like to me — that is, it feels like first being stimulated in a certain way and then keeping that stimulation going with an active mental response of mine. Furthermore, the fact that I can do this might well give me a sense of ownership over the process, and a sense of its occurring in a temporal present — in just the ways Humphrey suggests in connection with sensations. In fact, all that seems to be missing from this account of what my current state of attending is like is its *specific* character, as *an attending to the idea of a reverberant feedback loop*. Here, I think, we need to posit counterparts to the two properties of sensation that my current attending lacks, namely, bodily locatedness and sensory modality. Recall my bracketed remark under (4) above, that in Humphrey's own account the bodily location of a sensory stimulation is not literally a bodily location, but a site on a mental representation of the body. What is needed here is a site on an analogous mental representation — not a site on a mental representation of a body but, rather, a site within a represented mental space of contents or ideas. For then we can think of the specific object of my attending (in this case, the idea of a reverberant feedback loop) as being nailed down by the particular site in this mental space at which I am stimulated and to which I reach out with my response. The only other feature of my attending that needs to be nailed down is the fact that it is an attending — as opposed, say, to a wanting. And this can be handled analogously to Humphrey's way of handling sensory modality. He accounted for that by appealing to the idea that there are different ways or modes in which we can respond to stimulations when we reach out to them. Surely, this is a promising way to try to distinguish attending from wanting. If anything, it is a more promising way to cash out the differences between such propositional attitude types than it is a way of cashing out different sensory modalities. After all, it is independently plausible — that is, independently of Humphrey's account of phenomenal consciousness — that propositional attitudes are a species of action and, hence, that the differences among them might be cashed out as different ways or modes of acting. Whereas I don't think Humphrey can say that it is *independently* plausible that sensations are a species of action or that the differences among sensory modalities can be cashed out as different ways or modes of acting. These are suggestions that he has *made* plausible, by showing us just how much explanatory mileage we can get out of them.

How important is it that Humphrey's account of sensory consciousness is extendable in this way, to an alleged non-sensory case? Frankly, I'm not quite sure. But I want nonetheless to conclude by taking a provisional stand on this matter of the extent of phenomenal consciousness.

I said at the beginning that it is hard to see how disputes about its extent could ever be resolved, since the parties to the dispute can all claim to have first person authority about what's going on in their respective consciousnesses. I also said that I am uncertain why Humphrey is so sure that others are wrong when they claim to have phenomenal awareness of non-sensory states. But I can see why he might think he's on firmer ground than they. For, unless we go all the way with William James and insist that every mental item has its own distinctive qualitative aspect, then the onus is on us to say what distinguishes those items that have one from those that don't. And Humphrey at least has a clear position here. According to him, sensations are the only items that have a qualitative aspect, and they are distinguished by having all five of the properties in terms of which he characterizes what they're like. I myself am inclined to take a broader view of phenomenal consciousness than Humphrey but a narrower one than James. So the onus is on me to say what else, besides those five properties, might distinguish the mental items that have a qualitative aspect from those that don't. It's no accident that I chose as my (alleged) non-sensory case the case of attending. For, I would say that in my own case phenomenal awareness and attending seem to go together. Everything of which I am phenomenally aware is something I attend to, and nothing to which I don't attend is phenomenally present to me. This is hardly a new or radical idea. But it can be made radical by applying it to the case of sensations in such a way that it turns out to be possible to have sensations, including even pains, that one doesn't feel. Although some philosophers would say that this is a conceptual impossibility, I think it can happen. If one walks a long distance with a growing blister, one can make the pain 'go away' by concentrating on philosophical conversation. But I don't think one thereby takes the pain out of existence. One merely sends it outside the bounds of one's phenomenal awareness as those bounds are set by one's powers of attention. It might seem tautological to thus link phenomenal awareness with attending. But then at least it's not an error to do so; it's just uninformative. And this brings me to one reason why I find it significant that Humphrey's account of sensation can be extended so as to apply to the case of attending as well. In this way we get past tautology to something informative.

When I asked above whether it is important that Humphrey's account of phenomenal consciousness is extendable in this way, I confessed that I don't know. My own hunch is that it might be very important. Humphrey has asked, when and how did sentience emerge in evolutionary history? His answer is that it emerged when somatic responses on the part of primitive organisms to stimulations at their body surface came to have the five properties in terms of which he characterizes what sensations are like. When these properties are construed in a sufficiently abstract way, they can be seen as properties that sensations have in common with action. But, if I'm right, when the properties are construed in a sufficiently abstract way, they can also be viewed as properties that sensations have in common with attendings. And this puts us in a position to give the following answer to Humphrey's question: sentience emerged when organisms developed the capacity not only to respond to stimulations but, also, to *attend* to their responses. As I have portrayed this capacity, it is the capacity to literally hold something in mind — by setting up precisely the sorts of reverberant feedback loops that Humphrey posits in the case of sensations. I suspect that this capacity was first exercised in the way he suggests, in connection with the monitoring of somatic conditions that belongs to the function of sensations in particular. However, even his own way of describing the capacity brings out that from the start it involved highly internalized responses that were directed not to bodily conditions *per se* but to mental representations of them. And this leads me to suspect that from the start it may have emerged as a highly general capacity with a potentially broad range of application — the capacity to keep all sorts of mental occurrences going by means of feedback loops and, thereby, to literally hold them in one's mind. Whether such a general capacity for attention is important depends upon what *else* it would enable organisms to do. On introspective grounds, I would say that it gives one the time and opportunity to make more responses and more varied responses to whatever it is one is attending to — in other words, to think longer and harder about it. I'll also risk a slightly wilder speculation, which is that it also made a difference to the evolution of certain social capacities. For I suspect that the capacity to lock another organism's eyes in a mutual gaze is also provided for by the capacity to set up the right kinds of feedback loops: your gaze is a stimulation to which I respond by gazing at you, which in turn keeps your own gaze going and so on, and all the while we're both setting up internal feedback loops as well in order to attend to the idea of this feedback loop that we have set up between us. Whatever the merits of this wilder speculation, I hope it is clear why I have a hunch that finding a link between sentience and attention might well be important. Whereas Humphrey's evolutionary perspective leads him to emphasize what sensations have in common with their somatic ancestors, I would like to emphasize what they have in common with their mental descendants. In that way, we might make still further progress on the mind–mind problem to which Humphrey's account of sensation is already a significant contribution.

Robert Van Gulick

Closing the Gap?

Nicholas Humphrey's ambitiously titled paper (2000) falls into two main parts. In the first, he offers a diagnosis of the current state of the mind–body debate and a general prescription for how to go about seeking its solution. In the second, he aims to fill that prescription with a specific proposal that he regards as bringing us much closer to a resolution of the underlying problem. Though I will take issue below with a few important details, I largely agree with his diagnosis of the current debate. However, I remain sceptical about just how far his more specific suggestions can take us toward an adequate understanding of the brain–consciousness relation. Perhaps with more development, they might cut deeper to the core, but in present form they seem subject to the same sorts of objections that Humphrey himself raises against other prior proposals, for example, absent qualia challenges.

Consider first his diagnosis. Humphrey rightly notes that no amount of correlational evidence in itself — no matter how well confirmed — will suffice to answer the mind–body question. Correlations between brain states and particular sorts of conscious episodes may give us strong reason to believe *that* the one depends upon the other, but they don't in themselves give us an understanding of *how* the two sides fit together. Early in the history of contemporary physicalism, Herbert Fiegel (1958) noted the unacceptability of *nomological danglers:* law-like mind/body relations unsupported by any explanations in terms of more basic linkages. Following Joseph Levine (1983), the more recent debate often appeals to the alleged *explanatory gap* that still separates our mental and physical representations of reality. That gap is regarded as deeper and more baffling than other, more mundane, lacunae in our overall framework of theories (for example, between the genetic and the embryological). Here, supposedly, we confront a blank wall. According to Colin McGinn (1989), the arch-pessimist in Humphrey's survey, the link seems almost magical; how could one transform the water of brain into the wine of consciousness?

Almost all parties to the present debate would agree with Humphrey that our current understanding of the mind/body link has puzzling gaps — ones we don't at present know how to span (with Daniel Dennett [1991] as the most prominent likely dissenter, given his deflationary view of what needs to be explained). However, philosophers disagree strongly about our prospects for bridging the gap, and on this point, what Humphrey says may mislead a bit. He speaks of a 'philosophical consensus' about our negative prospects and equates it with McGinn's (1989) deeply pessimistic view according to which we humans lack the requisite cognitive and

Journal of Consciousness Studies, **7**, No. 4, 2000, pp. 93–7

conceptual capacities to make the link intelligible to ourselves. McGinn's view has generated a lot of discussion, but more often to attack it than endorse it. The majority position seems closer to that which Humphrey himself recommends: modest optimism about closing the gap by building out from both sides. Indeed, theorists as otherwise diverse as William Lycan (1996), Paul Churchland (1995), and Owen Flanagan (1992) propose doing just that. Indeed, it even has a name: Pat Churchland (1986) has dubbed it 'co-evolution', reflecting the way in which our conceptions and theories on both sides of the divide change over time as we bring them in correspondence. Thus, Humphrey's approach seems right, but closer to the norm than he might seem to suggest.

I have two other small reservations about Humphrey's description of the debate. First, he couches the link in terms of identity. For example, he says that we will not solve the problem, *'unless and until we can set out the identity in a way that meets certain minimum standards for explanatory possibility'* (p. 7; original emphasis). Indeed, he even implies (p. 6) that David Chalmers regards some mind–body relations as metaphysically primitive identities; that cannot be right since, as Humphrey notes, Chalmers is a property dualist. What he regards as primitive are not identities but nomic links between distinct (i.e. non-identical) mental and physical properties (1996).

For a variety of reasons philosophers now tend to frame the issue in terms of how the mental might be *realized* by or *logically supervene* upon the physical rather than in terms of identity (Kim, 1998). For example, the identity version runs afoul of the fact that the cross-temporal identity conditions for mental states typically differ from those of their physical basis states. If I form a memory of writing this sentence which I recall ten minutes from now and again two hours from now, there may be good psychological reasons for regarding the mental state as the same memory at both times, even if there have been non-trivial changes in the physical substrate over that interval. The identity conditions for *being the same mental state* do not necessarily track those for *being the same neural or physical state*. Thus real problems can arise if we frame the issue in terms of identity between states rather than in terms of the realization of properties at one level by those at another. Thus I think it would be better to reframe Humphrey's questions in terms of realization. The how-question we need to answer is: 'How can (the having of) a conscious experience be realized by an underlying neural/physical substrate?'

Humphrey also quickly dismisses the prospects for building explanatory links through the common two-step method of functional analysis and realization laws. Doing so would require us to give a functional account of phenomenal states and then show how those functional conditions might be satisfied by neural systems. Humphrey argues that no one has 'the least idea of how to characterize' experience in functional terms, and he notes the existence of 'well known arguments (for example, the Inverted Spectrum) that purport to prove that it cannot be done, even in principle' (p. 9). Although he does not explicitly endorse these arguments, he has nothing further to say about the functional strategy after this apparent dismissal.

This again strikes me as a bit too quick, and might leave readers with the impression that this is a settled question among philosophers. It is not. Granted many are sceptical about the possibility of functional analysis, but many others argue that the inadequacy of current functional models in no way rules out the possibility of giving more satisfactory ones in the future. Nor can one claim that any such model will be open to absent qualia objections without begging the question at issue: namely whether or not one can articulate a set of functional conditions that could be satisfied only by systems with genuine qualia (Van Gulick, 1992). The point is too large to argue here, but we should at least acknowledge the open state of play on the question.

Let us turn, then, to the second part of Humphrey's paper and his particular proposal for closing the gap. Humphrey rightly argues at the outset that we must take care to put the right items on the two sides of the gap if we are to have any hope of building an explanatory link. He puts the point in terms of 'dimensions'; both sides, he says, 'must have the same conceptual dimensions, which is to say they must belong to the same generic class' (p. 8). Though I find the talk of 'dimensions' here less than clear, I agree with Humphrey's basic point. Indeed I have argued for a similar requirement, which I call the 'right relata problem' (1999). Much of the perplexity that surrounds standard examples of mind/body linkage may indeed result from mismatching items of different categories on the two sides. However, one must be careful not to interpret the requirement too simplistically, especially if one is dealing with matters of realization rather than identity. In a case of identity, the items related are really just one item, and so, of course, there is no room for items of distinct categories. But in cases of realization, the underlying substrate need only endow the higher level item with its properties; it need not itself share those properties and indeed might be of a different category. What is crucial is that we can explain how the properties of the higher level item depend upon (or derive from) those of the underlying realization.

Humphrey refines his view of the mind-side component of the link through a series of steps, 'the phantasm of pain becomes the sensation of pain, the sensation of pain becomes the experience of actively paining, the activity of paining becomes the activity of reaching out to the body surface in a painy way, and this activity becomes self-resonant and thick' (p. 15). Via this progression, he claims to arrive at a characterization of the mental side of the divide that we can link to brain states in a way that dispels the air of magic. Two sorts of questions arise: how plausible is his account of the nature of sensation, and, if true, would it allow us to forge the needed explanatory mind/body links. I have worries about each.

Thomas Reid notwithstanding, I find it difficult to regard perception and sensation as independent to the degree Humphrey claims, especially if we are using the latter term to cover not just bodily feelings such as tickles and pains, but also other forms of experience with a phenomenal aspect, such as the having of a red visual experience. When I see the red coke can on the table before me, I don't seem to undergo two distinct processes, one of which concerns 'my actively reaching out to my body surface' (my retina perhaps?) and the other a 'judgment about the objective facts in the external world'. Rather, I experience the red as an intrinsic feature of the external soda can that appears before me on the table. Given philosophical or scientific reflection, I may come to a different view about the nature of the experienced colour, but from the inside, introspectively and phenomenologically, I experience it as a feature of the can out there on the table. If so, then it would seem that the phenomenal aspect, the sensuous aspect, is intimately bound up with the perceptual states in which it plays such a crucial role. Perhaps I lack that degree of attention needed to separate the two, which Reid in a passage quoted by Humphrey observes is 'not to be expected in the vulgar, and is even rarely found in philosophers' (p. 12). But I don't believe it is just a failure of discrimination on my part, and I would like to hear more from Humphrey about what's wrong with my introspectively based belief about the central role phenomenal properties play in my perceptual experience.

In Humphrey's 'just so' story, the 'two parallel channels' of sensation and perception arose and continued to evolve 'along relatively independent paths' (p. 17). If one is engaging in evolutionary speculation, it seems more likely that as perception developed into a means for acquiring and representing information about objective distal features, it might have co-opted the representational resources of the more proximal sensation system. On that story, qualia initially figured in sensation-like proximal representation but got recruited into a more distal perceptual role, as the organism's ability to acquire such external information grew. Of course, it's just speculation, but no more so than Humphrey's own 'just so' tale.

Other key aspects of Humphrey's story would also benefit from clarification. For example, how are we to cash the metaphor of 'reaching out to the body surface with an evaluative response'? When I experience a red soda can, in what way do I reach out to my body surface? Moreover, Humphrey argues that it is 'this efferent activity which I am aware of' (p. 13). But what evidence supports this claim? What argument overturns the more commonly held belief that what I am aware of is generated by the representational processing of the afferent or input stream? Humphrey's alternative is original and thought-provoking, but given its originality, one would like to hear more about why one should accept it and reject the prior consensus to the contrary.

Given the unclearness about how to unpack the details of the proposal (for example, the metaphor of reaching out to the surface), it is hard to say just how far it might go to bridge the psycho-physical gap. But insofar as the proposal is clear, it does not seem adequate to remove the residual mystery. Indeed, it seems open to the same sorts of objections raised in the literature against prior functionalist proposals. In particular, it seems open to absent qualia challenges. For example, let us concede, for sake of argument, two claims that figure prominently in Humphrey's account: that sensation involves an active efferent response and that it involves some sort of thick self-resonance. How would either help us bridge the psycho-physical divide? Couldn't one easily imagine systems responding to stimuli that exhibited both of those features but lacked any phenomenal awareness, any inner what's-it-like-to-be-ness. Such absent qualia cases certainly seem possible; couldn't one build all sorts of self-resonating circuits without producing phenomenal awareness. And the same would seem to be true for systems with active efferent responses that give rise to an awareness of themselves. If we read 'awareness' as 'phenomenal awareness' then of course one couldn't have an absent qualia system whose efferent responses generated awareness in that sense. But that would just beg the question. However, if we read 'awareness' in some more neutral sense, then it seems we could have absent qualia systems that were aware of their evaluative efferent responses. Simply imagine a robot that generates such responses to stimuli and monitors them. Such a system would seem to satisfy Humphrey's conditions, but that in itself would give us little reason to regard it as phenomenally conscious.

Perhaps I have misunderstood those conditions, and were I to grasp them more clearly, I would see how they entail phenomenal consciousness. If so, I hope Humphrey will spell out more explicitly just what those conditions are and how they suffice for consciousness, since as far as I see, they do not.

What, then, is the bottom line with respect to our two questions? On the empirical side it would seem we need more evidence to support Humphrey's claims about sensation, perception and the role of efferent activity in conscious awareness. As to closing the gap, Humphrey needs to spell out more explicitly just how his story, if true, would dissolve the residual mystery. He acknowledges that 'there are, of course, loose ends to this analysis and ambiguities' (p. 15). But that seems to understate the outstanding debt; it is not merely loose ends but the main moves that still need spelling out: how do we get the 'wine' of full blown subjective phenomenal consciousness from the processes he describes? As in his book *A History of the Mind* (1992), Humphrey's article is full of intriguing and original suggestions, pointing out new directions for investigation and probing deep beneath the surface. But also here as well, we are not given an account with enough articulation to see whether or how it might indeed help close the gap. I look forward to hearing more from Humphrey on this topic.

References

Chalmers, D.J. (1996), *The Conscious Mind* (Oxford: Oxford University Press).

Churchland, P.M. (1995), *The Engine of Reason, The Seat of the Soul* (Cambridge, MA: MIT Press).

Churchland, P.S. (1986), *Neurophilosophy* (Cambridge, MA: MIT Press).

Dennett, D.C. (1991), *Consciousness Explained* (New York: Little Brown).

Fiegel, H. (1958), 'The "mental" and the "physical"', in *Minnesota Studies in the Philosophy of Science II*, ed. H. Fiegel, G. Maxwell and M. Scriven (Minneapolis: University of Minnesota Press).

Flanagan, O. (1992), *Consciousness Reconsidered* (Cambridge, MA: MIT Press).

Humphrey, Nicholas (1992), *A History of the Mind* (London: Chatto & Windus).

Humphrey, N. (2000), 'How to solve the mind–body problem', *Journal of Consciousness Studies*, **7** (4), pp. 5–20 (this issue).

Kim, J. (1998), *Mind in a Physical World* (Cambridge, MA: MIT Press).

Levine, J. (1983), 'Materialism and qualia: The explanatory gap', *Pacific Philosophical Quarterly*, **64**, pp. 354–61.

Lycan, W. (1996), *Consciousness and Experience* (Cambridge, MA: MIT Press).

McGinn, C. (1989), 'Can we solve the mind–body problem?', *Mind*, **98**, pp. 349–66.

Van Gulick, R. (1992), 'Understanding the phenomenal mind: Are we all just armadillos?', in *Consciousness*, ed. M. Davies and G. Humphreys (Oxford: Basil Blackwell).

Van Gulick, R. (1999), 'Taking a step back from the gap', *Proceedings of the World Congress of Philosophy XX* (Boston).

Nicholas Humphrey

In Reply

> It is very difficult, now that everybody is so accustomed to everything, to give an idea of
> the kind of uneasiness felt when one first looked at all these pictures on these walls. . . .
> Now I was confused and I looked and I looked and I was confused.
>
> Gertrude Stein, on her reaction to first seeing Cubist paintings,
> *The Autobiography of Alice B. Toklas* (1961)

I heard Daniel Dennett, last year, winding up his Royal Institute of Philosophy Millennial Lecture with the prediction: 'I anticipate a day when philosophers and scientists and laypeople will chuckle over the fossil traces of our earlier bafflement about consciousness' (Dennett, in press). And I thought at the time: that's not quite right. Future philosophers won't *chuckle* over the difficulties we now have with understanding consciousness — any more than we, today, *chuckle* over the difficulties people had two centuries ago with understanding the evolution of life.

We chuckle when something is comical. But the spectacle of earnest seekers after truth trying their very best to make sense of something that is presently beyond their capacity is, I'd say, more chastening than comical. In the case of evolution, when we look back on the efforts of pre-Darwinian thinkers to understand the origins of biological design (including even such giants of their time as David Hume), their struggles seem both heroic and tragic. It's like watching the earliest attempts of climbers to climb Mount Everest without the help of oxygen.

Of course, ever since Darwin we have had access to the Big Idea — the idea of natural selection — which today allows every schoolchild to understand biological design, and which makes those earlier efforts look so footling and incompetent. Nonetheless, we should be clear about what is hidden in that phrase 'ever since Darwin'. Even though the idea of natural selection can now be summarised and explained in a few sentences, it did not in fact spring into existence all at once, nor from one source. The progress of ideas is almost never like that. In reality, so-called scientific revolutions are no more punctuated and discontinuous than is biological evolution itself: zoom in on the details and you will always find all sorts of false starts and in-between, half-baked stages on the way to the eventual solution. Darwin himself struggled over many years with his version of the theory. And even after its publication in 1859, the argument quite properly went on. Several key bits of the theory were not yet in place. The facts were not yet — at least not yet known to be — as they would have to be.

Now, in the case of consciousness, I see us as being at a very comparable stage of creation, confusion and backsliding, such as existed in the case of evolution in the

Journal of Consciousness Studies, **7**, No. 4, 2000, pp. 98–112

mid-nineteenth century. This is the time when another Big Idea — the idea of how to link the conscious mind and the material body — is in the very process of being thought-through, reworked and edited (although, in this case, since the age of Victorian Genius has passed, it is not being done by just one or two great men but by a whole community of us). I am optimistic enough to believe, as Dennett does, that in a hundred years time, the problem of consciousness will indeed have been finally resolved — so that our descendants may even be able to write the answer on a postcard. But (and here Dennett and I part company) I cannot say that we are there yet. Not quite. And meanwhile it's difficult. And worrying. And it hurts. And it sometimes seems we're getting nowhere — though in retrospect it will be obvious that we were.

My target paper in this issue and the commentaries on it do, I hope, make a contribution to the job in hand. The fact that every commentator has a different view of what's right and what's wrong with the paper (with one commentator's view of what's wrong being precisely another's of what's right) at least means we are in the zone of uncertainty where interesting things happen.

I wanted to keep the target paper short, and I justified this to myself by imagining that a good many readers might already have some familiarity with the book in which I treated several of the issues discussed here at much greater length (Humphrey, 1992). Or at any rate, I hoped readers might take the trouble to refer back to it. But I can see now that these assumptions were unrealistic, and that by failing to elaborate at several points within the paper I invited too much second-guessing as to what it was I meant (or should have meant): 'If I understand him' (when in fact she hasn't), 'Humphrey needs to provide more on this in future' (when in fact he has provided considerably more in the not so distant past), and so on.

One solution, now, might be to try to make amends for leaving so much in abeyance by quoting major chunks from *A History of the Mind* in this reply. But, as luck would have it, the need for this has been partly lifted by one of the existing commentators who, as if foreseeing my difficulty, has seen fit to provide a blow-by-blow account of how he himself read the argument of my earlier book. In fact Christian de Quincey's sensitive and detailed summary does the job so much better than I could have done myself, that I can only recommend to anyone who finds that my target paper moves too fast or too far for them that they should turn immediately to de Quincey pp. 67–82 above) for online help.

Still, I am well aware that some of the commentators have found faults with the paper that go far beyond any frustration they may have felt with simply not being able to see what I am getting at. Indeed, some have clearly seen precisely what I am getting at — and, the more they have seen, the less they have been inclined to agree with it. In what follows I shall address, in turn, four areas of serious disagreement. For reasons of space, I shall pass over the many other areas where commentators have had helpful and constructive things to say, because in these areas the commentaries speak for themselves.

I should confess, however, that, even as I begin this, I have a sinking feeling. The target paper was short because I wanted, for once, to tell the story quickly and simply without being obliged to fend off every well-worn (and not so well-worn) objection. But now, here I am, about to engage in some of the very arguments I hoped I could ride over. In the end, I would rather people remembered the target paper than this reply.

I: Sensation and Perception.

I say that when we talk about the central fact of consciousness — namely, the fact that it is *like something* to have certain experiences — we are (if we but knew it) talking always about the subjective experience of sensation. As I summed this up before (and I am, after all, going to quote here from the book, p. 115):

(1) To be conscious is essentially to have sensations: that is, to have affect-laden mental representations of something happening here and now to me.
(2) The subject of consciousness, 'I', is an embodied self. In the absence of bodily sensations 'I' would cease. *Sentio, ergo sum* — I feel therefore I am.
(3) All sensations are implicitly located at the spatial boundary between me and not-me, and at the temporal boundary between past and future: that is, in the 'present'.

Hence, if we are to pin down precisely what *kind* of thing phenomenal consciousness is, we must pin down what *kind* of thing sensation is. And this means, I claim, that we must take pains from the outset to recognize the essential difference between sensation and perception. Sensation has evolved specifically to represent and evaluate the current state of stimulation at the surface of the body, whereas perception has evolved to represent the objective facts about the world beyond. If anything is important to understanding consciousness *this distinction* is.

Now, the absolute separation between two things that are usually run together is, I know, not easy to come to terms with — whether at the level of personal phenomenology or at the level of the underlying psychology and neuroscience (if it were easy, it would not have needed the first fifteen chapters of my book to make the case for it). But I argue that this separation is supported — and indeed demanded — by a variety of lines of argument and evidence which together confirm that despite the fact that both sensation and perception rely on the same sense organs, the central channels that process them have developed along separate lines in evolution and still today are functionally and even neuroanatomically discrete.

Let's consider in some detail, since it seems to be the area where I am most often challenged, the case of *colour vision*. 'Seeing colour', according to this theory, usually consists in having not one kind of experience but two. From the moment light, reflected from an external object, arrives at the human eye, there are two kinds of analysis that get under way: one track — the sensory one — leads to a representation of the distribution, intensity and quality of light at the eye, whereas the other track — the perceptual one — leads to a representation of the reflectance properties of the object that gave rise to this light. The colour of the light can be designated as colour with a small c, and the surface Colour of the object as Colour with a big C.

What are the grounds, then, for the claim that colour sensation and Colour perception are separate and parallel processes (rather than being, as Robert van Gulick suggests they might equally be, all part of a single serial production)? I think the case can be argued at two levels, the analytical and the empirical. But it should be enough if I cite here some of the empirical evidence that the two kinds of representation can function independently.

The most dramatic evidence comes from cases of brain damage, where there can be a double dissociation between colour sensation and Colour perception. Thus, on the one hand, in some cases of colour agnosia, sensation is unaffected (so that the subject still experiences the full richness of what it's like to have colourful stimulation of his visual fields), while at the same time Colour perception is lost (so that he is no longer able to judge what the Colour of any particular object is) (Oxbury *et al.*, 1969). On the other hand, in cases of blindsight, Colour perception may be spared (so that the subject can still guess the Colour of an external surface), while colour sensation is lost (so that he now says it's not like anything to have stimulation of his visual fields, and indeed that he is no longer conscious of seeing anything at all) (Stoerig and Cowey, 1997).

But even when the brain is working normally, there is plenty to indicate that colour sensation and Colour perception are relatively separate operations. For example, the time courses are different, with sensation leading perception by a considerable margin. We have all experienced this when, say, the lights go up in a dark room full of coloured books, curtains, rugs. All at once we have the experience of a field full of colour sensation, but — as reaction time experiments show — it may be all of several seconds before we can bring the results of Colour perception to bear on identifying the Colour of a target object. With psychotropic drugs, this divergence can be amplified, with sensation overwhelming perception altogether. Thus, as Aldous Huxley described it:

> At ordinary times the eye concerns itself with such problems as *Where? — How far? — How situated in relation to what?* In the mescaline experience the implied questions to which the eye responds are of another order. Place and distance cease to be of much interest. The mind does its perceiving in terms of intensity of existence . . . . (Huxley, 1954).

But, on the other hand, there are situations where we perceive Colour without sensing colour at all, as for example in the phenomenon that Michotte drew attention to of the 'amodal completion of perceptual structure', when we perceive the Colour of the surface of an object which is temporarily covered by a black mask passing in front of it (Michotte *et al.*, 1964/1991; Natsoulas, 1999).

Further remarkable evidence comes from young children. It is well known that children are surprisingly slow to learn Colour names, so that long after they demonstrably respond attentionally to coloured light and show colour preferences, they still cannot, for example, label a tomato as Red or grass as Green. But even once Colour perception is firmly established, and the Colour words are there, it seems that the child may still not yet have put two and two together and have realized that she generally perceives Colour in the external world at the same time she senses colour at her eyes — with the result that there's a stage at which she simply does not appreciate that Colour perception is mediated by eyesight. Put a green squishy ball in a three-year-old child's hand and ask her what Colour it is, and she will look at it and say Green, or ask her whether it is hard or soft, and she will squeeze it and say Soft; but now put it in a bag and ask her what she would *have to do* either to find out what its Colour is or to find out whether it is Hard or Soft — would she have to put her hand in and feel it or would she have to take a look? — and she'll likely say she does not know the answer (O'Neill *et al.*, 1992). It's as if the contingent association between perception and sensation (the contingency that as adults we find it so hard not to regard as *necessary*), has for the toddler simply not yet been figured out.

Yet I realize that you may hear all this evidence, and still find it hard to accept the story as I tell it. Among the commentators, Robert van Gulick and Valerie Hardcastle are the most overtly suspicious of the validity of the distinction between sensation and perception. But it is clear from the scattered remarks of several others that they, too, either do not really buy it (even my best ally, Dennett, will only concede that 'something like' this distinction needs to be drawn), or at any rate that they have not understood just how strictly I think it needs to be applied.

In particular, people continue to have trouble with my insistence that the right way to describe it is as a distinction between the representation of 'what is happening to me' and of 'what is happening out there'. Even if they can see how this may be an appropriate description in the case of the proximal senses such as touch or taste, they cannot see how it can be appropriate in the case of the distal senses of vision and audition. And almost everyone seems to baulk at the idea — which remains absolutely central to my account — that *visual sensations* really are to do with representing 'what's happening *to me at my eyes*'. Van Gulick, for example, protests that when he looks at a red Coke can on the table, it seems to him he experiences the phenomenal colour 'as a feature of the can out there on the table' not as something happening to himself; and Hardcastle baldly states 'we don't feel redly about parts of our visual field . . . we project our visual sensations as something external to us'.

I agree, it usually *seems* like that to me as well. But we have to pursue this example further. Let's suppose that van Gulick now walks towards the table and brings his face close up to the Coke can, so that the can's image fills more and more of his visual field, until he is so close that all he sees is a red blur. The sensation is undergoing a major transformation. But while this is happening, is he perceiving any change in the 'features of the can out there on the table'? No, the change in sensation represents a change not in the can out there but only in the *image* of the can. And whose image is this, if not *van Gulick's* image? And where is it located, if not *at van Gulick's eyes*?

Whenever people come back to me with this objection, and repeat that it just does not *seem* to be the way I'm telling it: that visual sensations don't *seem* to be located at the eye (or auditory sensations at the ear, or olfactory sensations at the nose, etc.), I am inclined to ask them: So, what precisely would it seem like if they *were* located at eye (or the ear or the nose, etc.)? In the case of the eye, wouldn't you expect, for example, that the sensation of a coloured patch would in fact seem to grow larger when the eye got closer to the light source? Or that the sensation would shift when you pressed with a finger on the eyeball? Or that it would change colour when you donned dark glasses? and so on. In other words, wouldn't you expect it to be just like it is, like this!

II: 'Agentic Qualia'

My view, as expressed in this paper, about the limits of sensation (and of consciousness) is a purist one: namely that sensation always has to do with representing what's happening at the boundary between me and not me — which is to say at the body surface as mapped by sense organs. To continue the litany, from where I summarized things in my book (p. 116):

(4) For human beings, most sensations occur in the province of one of the five senses (sight, sound, touch, smell, taste). Hence most human states of consciousness have one or other of these qualities. There are no non-sensory, amodal conscious states.

(5) Mental activities other than those involving direct sensation enter consciousness only in so far as they are accompanied by 'reminders' of sensation, such as happens in the case of mental imagery and dreams.

(6) This is no less true of conscious thoughts, ideas, beliefs, [perception]. . . Conscious thoughts are typically 'heard' as images of voices in the head — and without this sensory component they would drop away.

However, here I am ready to make concessions. I was already becoming unsure of how far I really wanted to insist on this degree of purity even at the time I wrote this paper (and indeed the '*most* sensations' and '*most* human states of consciousness', in (4) above, indicate that I was hedging on it even earlier). And, now, both Ralph Ellis and Natika Newton, in their commentaries, help me see more clearly what is wrong with ruling out the possibility of there being *any* source of phenomenal consciousness other than conventional sensation.

What Ellis and Newton draw attention to is that there may in fact be a phenomenology of *action per se*. My claim in the paper is that, while it is 'like something' to have sensations, it is not like anything much to engage in most other bodily activities:

> To say the least, our experience of other bodily activities is usually very much shallower. When I wave my hand there may be, perhaps, the ghost of some phenomenal experience. But surely what it's like to wave hardly compares with what it's like to feel pain, or taste salt or sense red (p. 14, above).

Yet Ellis and Newton both say that this is wrong, because in reality it always does feel like something to be acting (or, as we shall see, even preparing to act). And I would now agree with them that it is at least partly wrong — the ghost is more substantial than I allowed!

I refer readers to the good discussion of the phenomenology of action that these authors (and Naomi Eilan, too) provide. But I have another reason for wanting to pursue the issue here: which is so that I can confront — and I hope deal with — a problem that no commentator has actually brought up on this occasion, but that I have had raised with me by others (especially John Searle). It's a problem that might otherwise prove to be the Achilles heel of the whole thesis about consciousness and sensations. (Some of what follows is from Humphrey, 2000b).

Suppose it were indeed true, as I maintained in a strong form above, that the entire content of consciousness is made up of bodily sensations, with nothing being contributed by perceptions or thoughts as such. It would follow presumably that a person will not experience any change in consciousness *unless* there is a change in sensation, even if there *is* a change in what is perceived or thought. But then consider what this means in the case, say, of vision. It has to mean that when someone is looking at a scene, he should experience no change in consciousness unless and until the visual stimulus as such changes (so as to create a change in 'what's happening to me'), even if he does come to perceive it differently in terms of what it represents as 'what's happening out there'. And, in that case, a crucial test would be provided by of one of those notorious ambiguous pictures, such as the Necker cube or the duck/rabbit, where, even though there is no change in the visual image, the perception of what it represents can indeed radically alter.

At a recent conference Searle challenged me directly about such cases, saying that, for example, it was perfectly obvious to him that the Necker cube seen in one way really is a consciously different phenomenon from the same cube seen the other way — thus proving, in contradiction to my own position, that we can in fact be conscious of what is perceived as well as of what is sensed.

Well, can we? I admit on the evidence of introspective observation the answer must be: Yes. When the cube reverses in depth there is surely *something* that consciously changes. And it certainly is not at the level of sensation of the visual image (which, *qua* represented image, does not even have a depth dimension to reverse).

What is this something, then? When the cube reverses, is there, as Searle would want to say, a change in some aspect of *non-sensory* perceptual consciousness — perhaps the coming and going of 'cube qualia'? (Just as, with the duck/rabbit, he might want to postulate the coming or going of 'duck qualia' or 'rabbit qualia'? I am not joking: some theorists are really prepared to talk this way.) If so, my argument is lost.

Or is there perhaps another possibility (as would surely be suggested by Eilan, Ellis and Newton)? When the cube reverses, is there a change not in non-sensory qualia nor in visual qualia but in *sensory qualia of another non-visual kind*? I believe there are in fact two ways that this could be happening.

One way of understanding it would be to take up an idea of the psychoanalyst Mark Solms (which he himself attributes to Freud), and to suggest that conscious experience is comprised not only of the five basic modalities of sensory qualia but also of an additional dimension of *affect*. 'Affective qualia', Solms writes, '(which are calibrated in degrees of pleasure/unpleasure) are wholly equivalent to the qualia of vision, hearing, smell, etc. and are irreducible to them' (Solms, 1997, p. 773). So, whenever we experience a sight or a sound or a taste, etc., perhaps the conscious experience is likely to consist *both* of the specific sensory qualia *and* of whatever affective qualia are being activated. But, while the sensory qualia are fixed solely by the sensory stimulus, the affective qualia may be influenced not only by the stimulus but also by what is being perceived. With an ambiguous figure, then, even though the visual sensation remains constant, when the perception changes the affective qualia may change too.

I think this is a nice idea, and in some cases it might be correct. But I am not sure it will do in general. Different affective feelings for ducks and rabbits? Well, why not. But different feelings for the two versions of the Necker cube? Unlikely.

The other way would be to take up the idea that Eilan, Ellis and Newton all hint at in their commentaries (and which I have in fact toyed with myself in earlier writings), and to suggest that what is crucial is not so much affect as *action*. Suppose that whenever we perceive anything (and sometimes even when we merely think of things) we always implicitly formulate a plan of action — for example a plan to reach out and take hold of it. And suppose that such action, even when implicit, always has a small but noticeable qualitative feel to it — either on its own account via somatic sensation or through modelling of the sensory feedback that would be expected. Let's call this additional dimension the dimension of 'agentic qualia' (Humphrey, 2000b). Then, whenever we experience a sight or a sound or a taste, etc., the conscious experience can be expected to consist not only of the sensory qualia appropriate to the particular sensation but also of whatever agentic qualia are being called into being by the perceived 'affordance for action' (in J.J. Gibson's terms).

This solves the problem of the Necker cube. For, now we can postulate that, even while the visual sensation remains constant, there may be a covert change in action plan when the perception of the cube reverses, and so a slight change in the overall sensory qualia. And of course it also solves much else that might otherwise be puzzling.

The admission of a realm of agentic qualia makes the story I have been telling considerably more complicated. But that's a good price to pay for making it more likely to be right.

One particular area, I might mention, in which it makes it more likely to be right — and indeed makes it possible to tell a story at all — is in relation to the much-disputed phenomenology of blindsight. Suppose that, despite the fact a person with blindsight has no consciousness of visual sensations in the blind field, he nonetheless does experience it as 'like something', consciously, to detect an object in the blind field (and several reports suggest that in a strange way it *may* be so) — then perhaps the explanation is that what he is experiencing are the agentic qualia associated with his having an incipient plan to grasp the object.

III: 'Mongrel' Phenomena

In Block's 1995 paper where he attempts to distinguish two concepts of consciousness — 'phenomenal' and 'access' consciousness — he remarks that the term consciousness as used in common parlance is a 'mongrel concept' (Block, 1995). Yet his choice of the word 'mongrel' for this is not quite right. A true mongrel concept would surely be one where two different parent concepts have been combined in one offspring, which as a result essentially has parts of both. But what Block has in mind is something less than this. He wants to say that the term consciousness typically bundles together several different concepts in a way that makes for problems in telling which particular concept is being referred to; but he does not want to say that these different concepts essentially belong together as a union.

Now, as Eilan points out, Block's distinction between phenomenal and access consciousness has an obvious affinity to my own distinction between sensation and perception — in fact, as I myself have said, it often amounts to being the very same distinction (Humphrey, 1995). And there is a parallel, too, in the way I, like Block, have seen it as the first task of a theory of consciousness to unbundle and lay out for separate view these two relatively autonomous concepts. Yet at various times I admit I have entertained a different thought: namely, that consciousness really might, after all, be a phenomenon that truly is a mongrel — such that you have to have *both* sensation *and* perception united in a single mental state to yield the real thing.

This same thought has clearly occurred to several of the commentators (in particular Eilan), who variously suggest ways in which sensation and perception may intimately depend on each other. But in the end I am not persuaded either by my own moves in this direction or theirs. I do believe that sensation can help to make perception a success for the perceiver; sensation can even be what makes us think (wrongly) of perception as having its own conscious phenomenology; but in the final analysis the two processes remain two, not one.

Still, let me at least soften my position, and hold a hand out in Eilan's direction. For I would say she has identified what is the most important way in which sensation can contribute to perception, which is by adding the crucial element of *presentness*. Indeed I (Humphrey, 1992), Anthony Marcel (1988) and Richard Gregory (1996) have all, in different ways, proposed the same idea: namely, that sensations are required, in Gregory's felicitous wording, 'to flag the present'.

The basic idea here is that one of the main (and, in evolution, ongoing) roles that sensation plays is, as I put it in the paper, to 'police' perception — or to help 'keep perception honest' (Humphrey, 2000a).

The reasoning is as follows. Both sensation and perception, as noted above, take sensory stimulation as their starting point: yet, while sensation then proceeds to represent the stimulation more or less as given, perception takes off in a much more complex and risky way. Perception has to combine the evidence of stimulation with contextual information, memory and rules so as to construct a hypothetical model of the external world as it exists independently of the observer. Yet the danger is that, if this kind of construction is allowed simply to run free, without being continually tied into present-tense reality, the perceiver may become lost in a world of hypotheticals and counterfactuals.

So, what the perceiver needs is the capacity to run some kind of online reality check, testing his perceptual model for its currency and relevance, and in particular keeping tabs on where he himself now stands. But this, so the argument goes, is in fact precisely where low level, unprocessed, sensation does prove its value. As I summarized it earlier: 'Sensation lends a here-ness and a now-ness and a me-ness to the experience of the world, of which pure perception in the absence of sensation is bereft' (Humphrey, 1992, p. 73).

Thus, here I am agreeing with Eilan. At the very least sensation is needed to establish the present-tense credentials of perception — and thereby, as it were, to license perception for use as a trustworthy representation of what's really out there *at this moment*. In fact, as Eilan might have hoped, I have long argued for the idea of *presence* as the defining phenomenon of conscious life, even to the extent of my developing the pun implicit in the word:

> The very word 'present' comes from the Latin *prae- sens*. *Prae* means 'in front of' and *sens* is the present participle of *sum* ('I am'). But *sens* is also the root of the past participle of *sentio* ('I feel'). Thus *sens* hovers ambiguously between 'being' and 'feeling', and *prae-sens* carries the implication of 'in front of a feeling being'. Correspondingly, the subjective present is comprised by what a person feels happening to him; and when he ceases having sensations — as when he enters dreamless sleep or dies — his present ends (Humphrey 1992, p. 99).

Even so, I will not, on this basis, go all the way with Eilan or anyone else to concluding that perception and sensation belong together as a single package. The reason is first, though I say it again, that perception and sensation are *about* different kinds of thing — so that, when it comes to it, the putative mongrel would not be the kind of within-category mongrel (say a spaniel-collie) that at least in principle makes sense, but a cross-category one (say a spaniel-tulip) that does not. And second, and in the end more telling, the reason is the one already described above, which is that in reality sometimes we can and sometimes we do experience sensation and perception independently. Perception without sensation, as in blindsight, is rare and certainly not normal — indeed it lacks precisely that *presence*, the hereness and nowness and me-ness, that sensation usually lends it. But visual perception in blindsight still works at the level of representing 'what's happening out there'.

If anyone who knows about human cases of blindsight should doubt me about this — perhaps because they are struck by the lack of visual spontaneity that human patients with partial blindsight show — I would refer them to my own study of a monkey, known as Helen, with complete blindsight after surgical ablation of the entire primary visual cortex. Helen's visually guided behaviour recovered to such a degree that anyone who observed her freely using her eyes to navigate through her environment would have assumed (quite rightly in my view) that her visual perception was almost back to normal (Humphrey, 1974; and see my discussion in 1992, pp. 88–93).

There is something else that the human blindsight patient lacks (and the monkey too, presumably), that is highly relevant to this discussion: when the patient engages in visual perception he does not experience it as *vision*. Instead he typically says that the experience has no modality at all. (Or, he may even become confused. A patient with the analogous syndrome in the tactile sphere — 'unfeeling touch' — while having no conscious tactile sensations, could nonetheless identify where he was being touched on his arm: but, when asked how he could do it, he would variously say he smelt or heard the stimulus (Paillard *et al.*, 1983)!)

In the monkey's case I had direct evidence that she, too, did not immediately recognise her capacity to use her eyes as a case of *vision*, when I found that early on her way to full recovery she actually muddled up lights with sounds. Thus, for example, after she had been trained to reach to touch a flashing light presented in the dark on the end of a stick, she immediately transferred to reaching for a clicking speaker on a stick, and it was only with difficulty that I could teach her to respond to the light and *not* the sound; what's more, when given a light and a speaker placed close together she sometimes reached between them (Humphrey, 1968; 1995).

This lack of awareness of the modality of a perceptual channel is just what we should expect of perception without sensation. But of course it draws attention to a further role that sensation normally plays in helping make perception a success. *Sensation tells the perceiver in what manner he is doing his perceiving.* In fact I might well have added a further '-ness' to the list above: 'Sensation lends a here-ness, a now-ness, a me-ness *and a modalness* to the experience of the world, of which pure perception in the absence of sensation is bereft'.

Yet I am afraid Andy Clark will not like this. For in his commentary he addresses this very same issue of how the modality of perceptions gets to be appreciated — and comes up with an entirely different answer. His own proposal is that the '[perceiving] agent has direct unmediated access to distinctive non-phenomenal properties of the act of detection itself. Where such access is available, the agent must judge there to be a difference in what it is like to gather information by sight rather than by, for example, hearing.' So, according to Clark, the modality of perceptions comes, in effect, free with the territory: the unique style of information processing involved in representing sights (as against sounds, say), and/or the types of affordances that sights (as against sounds) offer, intrinsically mark out visual perception as being qualitatively different from auditory perception — and no recourse to the modalness of accompanying sensations is necessary.

Clark says he is putting forward this suggestion in the context of my paper in order to be helpful to me. He thinks my theory is in trouble without it, because he does not see how modal quality — whether in the case of perceptions or sensations — can arise in any other way than the kind of way that he suggests. I am sorry if I seem ungrateful in saying Thanks but No Thanks for this offer of help. But I reckon I not only can but must manage without it. For I have to say I think his theory, as a theory of how perception gets to be tagged intrinsically as belonging to a particular modality, just cannot be right — for the simple reason that perception is *not* tagged intrinsically with a modality. Indeed, as we have seen, the reality is the reverse: perception is intrinsically *amodal*.

If Clark were right, several of the phenomena of amodal perception discussed above could simply never occur. It would be impossible for a person (or a monkey) with blindsight to perceive the shape or location of an object *without* appreciating the visualness of the experience. It would be impossible for a child to discover the Colour of a ball, *without* realising that she had used her eyes to do so. Or, to give one more remarkable example, it would be impossible for someone to use tactile stimulation on the skin as a basis for 'seeing' *without* this touch-driven experience taking on the phenomenal quality of vision. But in the case of such so-called 'skin vision', where someone has an optical image from a head-mounted camera translated into a pattern of tactile stimulation on the skin of their back, and proceeds to learn to use this pattern to 'see' with, in fact the sensory experience remains firmly tactile (Bach-y-Rita, 1972).

Actually, I do not want to dismiss Clark's theory altogether. Because I believe that, with a little negotiation, he and I would find that, after all, we are basically thinking on similar lines. It is just that Clark is using his theory to bark up the wrong tree. The place to which he ought to be applying this idea of there being direct unmediated access to phenomenal qualities is not perception (which is not intrinsically modal) but sensation (which *is*). And this is precisely where I myself — although Clark has clearly not read me this way — have tried to apply a very similar idea: namely, that phenomenal quality, and indeed phenomenal consciousness as a whole, is the direct and unmediated outcome of a certain, modality-specific, *way of doing things*.

IV: Functionalism and Zombie-Free Zones

Van Gulick takes me to task for saying in the paper: 'No one, it seems, has the least idea how to characterize the phenomenal experience of redness in functional terms. . . in fact there are well-known arguments (such as the Inverted Spectrum) that purport to prove that it cannot be done, even in principle.' 'Although [Humphrey] does not explicitly endorse these arguments,' van Gulick writes, 'he has nothing to say about the functional strategy after this apparent dismissal.' Hardcastle clearly sees me not as a functionalist but as a physicalist (or why else should she go on about whether my theory accords with the *anatomy*?). Meanwhile Clark, trying to see the brighter side, says he thinks that everything I say is in fact 'compatible with the claim being pitched at a functional, rather than a brute physical, level'.

But I am amazed. I took it for granted that everyone would recognize that my account of sensations was indeed meant to be a functional one through and through — so much so that I actually deleted the following sentences from an earlier draft of the paper, believing them redundant:

> Thus [with this account] we are well on our way to doing the very thing it *seemed* we would not be able to do, namely giving the mind term of the identity, the phantasm, a *functional description* — even if a rather unexpected and peculiar one. And, as we have already seen, once we have a functional description we're home and dry, because the same description can quite well fit a brain state.

But perhaps I should not be amazed. Functionalism is a wonderfully — even absurdly — bold hypothesis, about which few of us are entirely comfortable.

Bertrand Russell famously said: 'The method of "postulating" what we want has many advantages; they are the same as the advantages of theft over honest toil' (Russell, 1919). And it's only natural to wonder whether functionalism is theft, whereas only physicalism represents honest toil.

Even the most ardent functionalists (among whom I would include myself) seem sometimes not to appreciate just what it is their metaphysical position commits them to. This is that, if and when you've provided a functional account of everything you've been asked to account for — let's say everything that distinguishes a person who is having a red sensation — you've done the job and you can stop. There is no explanatory residue. At that point the objections are (like Monty Python's parrot) dead, kaput, ex-objections, objections that have gone to another place.

Michael Frayn stated the case for functionalism plainly in his novel, *The Tin Men* (Frayn, 1965). In this story, Macintosh, who is master of computers, is programming his computers to pray — or to engage in 'automated devotion', as he calls it. But a sceptical colleague objects that the difference is that a man who prays would *mean* it. Macintosh replies:

> So does the computer. Or at any rate, it would take a damned complicated computer to say the words without meaning them. I mean, what do we mean by 'mean'? If we want to know whether a man or a computer means 'O Lord, bless the Queen and her Ministers', we look to see whether it's grinning insincerely or ironically as it says the words. We try to find out whether it belongs to the Communist party. We observe whether it simultaneously passes notes about lunch or fornication. If it passes all the tests of this sort, what other tests are there for telling if it means what it says?

Now, I would agree that the problem of prayer is arguably an 'easy problem', compared to the 'hard problem' of seeing red. And I am not claiming that we yet have a functional account of sensation that passes *all* the tests. But, arguably, we do have an account that already passes *most* of the tests and that looks as if it is at least *on course* to pass the rest of them. Yet, among my colleagues commenting on this paper, it seems that the majority instead of declaring at least provisional success, cannot but have fits of self doubt. As Robert Pirsig wrote in *Zen and the Art of Motorcycle Maintenance*: 'The truth comes knocking on the door. And you say "Go away. I'm looking for the truth". And so it goes away' (Pirsig, 1974).

It's true that I have Newton on board with me. And Ellis and de Quincey are at least ready to sail alongside. But Clark is disappointing in this regard. Although, as I've indicated, I count him a friend to my approach, I'm dismayed to find him claiming that one of the key ideas — the idea that the subject is the 'author' of his own sensations — cannot deliver what I want, while Clark completely mistakes how I am supposing that this works.

'The mere idea of knowledge of authorship,' Clark writes, 'fails to illuminate the question of phenomenal feel. . . . Why should knowledge of authorship not be as free of sensational depth and character as, say, knowledge that Paris is the capital of France?' But the idea of 'knowledge' of authorship plays no role in my theory. Sensing does not involve 'knowledge' of sensing, any more than willing involves 'knowledge' of willing. In my view, what makes for phenomenal feel is *authorship as such*. To feel just *is* to be the author of a certain kind of response — and that's how and why the properties are self-disclosing.

I like Clark's notion of a 'necessarily zombie-free zone, a zone where facts about access imply (but do not assume) a difference in how things are sensationally given'. But I hoped he would see that my theory as it stands (without his revisions) already has the potential to lead into this zone.

Let me make a related point about authorship in reply to Hardcastle, who complains that she needs 'a way to distinguish, from the brain's point of view, conscious experience from the rest'. Her implicit suggestion that the brain *has* a point of view is of course a rather strange and interesting one. But again I hoped she would see that this is something I have already provided for, by making authorship central to the theory. Minds *and* brains can both in principle be authors — and authors do intrinsically have points of view.

I have to admit that, as van Gulick says, with this part of the theory there is a big IOU outstanding. The idea of authorship and all that follows from it still requires technical explication far beyond what I have yet provided. But I did at least make a start on it in my book, by trying to develop the idea of 'instructions' and recursive intentionality (see de Quincey's summary). Ten years later I suspect there are useful insights to be gleaned from the newly invented field of 'consumer semantics' according to which 'the intentional content of a state depends, at least in part, on what the downstream consumer systems which can make use of that state are disposed to do with it' (Carruthers, 2000) — which is just my earlier point. And I'm sure the other way to go with it, as Ellis persuasively argues in his commentary, will be to borrow ideas from dynamical systems theory to explain the very nature of agency.

It will not, now, be me who does it. But some day soon I have no doubt that others with superior technical skills will be able to set this notion of an 'author' on a solid analytic footing. It will then take its due place as a key — probably *the* key — 'dual currency concept' in the philosophy of mind. Indeed, perhaps it will turn out to be that oh-so-obvious big idea that future generations will be able to write down on a postcard — and to flourish in front of their benighted grandparents who once struggled to see how anything could be both mental *and* physical, and who lived in fear of 'absent qualia' and 'zombies'.

So, seriously, what about those zombies? There's no question that the anxiety, that Dennett (2000) calls the 'zombic hunch', continues to haunt the field. In fact it is clearly still there in the background of many if not all the present commentaries. Even those who are trying to kick the habit cannot, it seems, quite leave zombies alone.

Van Gulick is open about his continuing concern. Having declared himself — after some appropriate and helpful reservations — largely in favour of the approach I've taken, nonetheless he all of a sudden raises the spectre of 'absent qualia'.

> Couldn't one easily imagine systems [that had all the specified features] but lacked any phenomenal awareness, any inner what's-it-like-to-be-ness. . . . Simply imagine a robot that generates such responses to stimuli and monitors them. Such a system would seem to satisfy Humphrey's conditions, but that in itself would give us little reason to regard it as phenomenally conscious.

Van Gulick is of course entitled to question, at a scientific level, whether the specific features of my model are the right ones, so that implementing *those* features in a robot would make the robot conscious. (Although, be it said, as Dennett points out here, and as I discuss at some length in the book, that my model provides no simple blueprint for wiring up consciousness *de novo*: it is a model of how the functional pathways *developed in the course of evolution*, and no one is going to be able to implement these details without retracing much of the evolutionary history.) All the same, I do not think I am misreading van Gulick when I say I detect, in his statement 'perhaps were I to grasp [the conditions] more clearly I would see how they entail phenomenal consciousness', not so much a judicious withholding of judgement as a reluctance to believe that anything I or anyone else could offer would *ever* do the trick.

At a different level, I guess de Quincey is a closet zombist too. He goes further than van Gulick in declaring his support for what I'm doing (in fact he goes further than anyone, bar Dennett), but then he, too, suddenly jumps ship. He says that, at the last moment in my evolutionary story, I have helped myself to the idea of the 'subjective present', when nothing in the functional account of subjectivity that I was developing entailed it. The implication is that we could have everything that my model does entail, without there being a phenomenal 'present'. But, since as we all know subjectively, the fact is there *is* a phenomenal present, this means that the potential for presentness was already latent in the design of the universe and has to be considered primitive — at least as a primitive *potential*. And for de Quincey (rather as for Chalmers) this clearly has to be a contingent fact about the universe, not a necessary one: logically it could have been otherwise (Van Gulick is right to correct me about what I said about Chalmers' position in the paper).

I do not know how to respond to this: except to say okay, but then show me how there could be the functional states in place but *not* the presentness. The idea of there being unrealized *potential* in the universe is of course basic to functionalist metaphysics. Thus we all agree there must have been, for example, the potential for there being 'square roots' and 'justice' and the '*Journal of Consciousness Studies*', and so on, long before the requisite functional states were ever realized. But, once they *were* realized, then surely these things had to exist necessarily. And the same for phenomenal consciousness and the subjective present. There's nothing contingent about it. I and you are conscious, not contingently, but *necessarily*.

Sometimes, I confess, that when faced with the only-up-to-a-point functionalism of van Gulick or de Quincey or most of my colleagues, I am almost relieved to come across the unrepentant in-your-face *anti-functionalism* of Stevan Harnad. At least with Harnad you know where you are. The sarcasm is transparent: 'I can design and implement recursive self-sustaining loops fitting Humphrey's description easily. Do they quicken with the light of consciousness?' No of course not, because: 'If we "characterize" feelings computationally or functionally, we have simply begged the question, and changed the subject'. Functionalism for Harnad is by definition 'zombie functionalism'.

But, if I am glad to have Harnad state the enemy's case so boisterously and scornfully as he does in his commentary, it's only because he thereby reveals the ultimate vacuity of his position. It goes nowhere. It makes no predictions. It generates no tests. Indeed, for Harnad it would actually be an argument against the legitimacy of any theory of consciousness that someone should even imagine that his theory could be *tested* by implementing the consciousness-producing architecture *in a machine*. Because if he were to interpret anything the machine actually *does* with its new architecture (anything at all) as evidence that the implementation has been successful, that would only show that his theory begged the question.

It's as though Harnad has managed to turn Tertullian's grand claim 'I believe because it is impossible' into its corollary 'I do not believe because it *is* possible'.

Of course this was also the ultimate argument used against Darwin. It may be true, the churchmen said, that it would have been *possible* for the living world to have been designed by natural selection. But don't be fooled. God has arranged things to appear *as-if* designed by natural selection, just so as to test your faith in the fact that they have *not really* been so designed.

A hundred and fifty years later no one can be bothered with such sophistry. And there's a moral there.[1]

References

Bach-y-Rita, P. (1972), *Brain Mechanisms in Sensory Substitution* (London: Academic Press).

Block, N. (1995), 'On a confusion about a function of consciousness', *Behavioral and Brain Sciences*, **18**, pp. 227–47.

Carruthers, P. (2000), 'Replies to critics: Explaining subjectivity', *Psyche*, **6**, (3).

Dennett, D.C. (2000), 'The zombic hunch: Extinction of an intuition?', *Philosophy*, in press.

Frayn, M. (1965), *The Tin Men* (Boston: Little, Brown and Co.).

Gregory, R.L. (1996), 'What do qualia do?', *Perception*, **25**, pp. 377–8.

Humphrey, N.K. (1968), *Two Studies in the Neuropsychology of Vision*, PhD thesis, University of Cambridge.

Humphrey, N.K. (1974), 'Vision in a monkey without striate cortex: A case study', *Perception*, **3**, pp. 241–55.

Humphrey, N. (1992), *A History of the Mind* (London: Chatto & Windus).

Humphrey, N. (1995), 'Blocking out the distinction between sensation and perception: Superblindsight and the case of Helen', *Behavioral and Brain Sciences*, **18**, pp. 257–8.

Humphrey, N. (2000a), 'The privatization of sensation', in *The Evolution of Cognition*, ed. C. Heyes and L. Huber (Cambridge, MA: MIT Press), in press.

Humphrey, N. (2000b), 'Now you see it, now you don't', [commentary on Crick and Koch, 2000], *Neuro-Psychoanalysis*, **2**, in press.

Huxley, A. (1954), *The Doors of Perception* (New York: Harper and Row).

Marcel, A.J. (1988), 'Phenomenal experience and functionalism', in *Consciousness in Contemporary Science*, ed. A.J. Marcel, and E. Bisiach (Oxford: Clarendon Press).

Michotte, A., Thinés, G. and Crabbé, G. (1964/1991), 'Amodal completion of perceptual structures', in *Michotte's Experimental Phenomenology of Perception*, ed. G. Thinés, A. Costall and G. Butterworth (Hillsdale, NJ: Erlbaum).

Natsoulas, T. (1999), 'A rediscovery of presence', *Journal of Mind and Behavior*, **20**, pp. 17–42.

O'Neill, D.K., Astington, J.W. and Flavell, J.H. (1992), 'Young children's understanding of the role sensory experience plays in knowledge acquisition', *Child Development*, **63**, pp. 474–90.

Oxbury, J.M., Oxbury, S.M. and Humphrey, N.K. (1969), 'Varieties of colour anomia', *Brain*, **92**, pp. 847–60.

Paillard, J., Michel, F. and Stelmach, G. (1983), 'Localization without content: A tactile analogue of "blindsight"', *Archives of Neurology*, **40**, pp. 548–51.

Pirsig, R. (1974), *Zen and the Art of Motorcycle Maintenance* (London: Bodley Head).

Russell, B. (1919), *Introduction to Mathematical Philosophy* (London: Allen and Unwin).

Solms, M. (1997), 'What is consciousness?', *Journal of the American Psychoanalytical Association*, **45**, pp. 681–703.

Stein, G. (1961), *The Autobiography of Alice B. Toklas* (New York: Random House).

Stoerig, P. and Cowey, A. (1997), 'Blindsight in man and monkey', *Brain*, **120**, pp. 535–59.

---

[1] Carol Rovane's commentary, which provides a particularly perceptive and constructive critique of the target paper, unfortunately arrived after this reply had been completed.

CYBERNETICS
& HUMAN KNOWING

a journal of second-order cybernetics, autopoiesis and cyber-semiotics

CYBERNETICS
& HUMAN KNOWING
a journal of second-order cybernetics
autopoiesis and cyber-semiotics
10, No.3-4,

Heinz von Foerst

CYBERNETICS
& HUMAN KNOWING
a journal of second-order cybernetics
autopoiesis and cyber-semiotics
Volume 13, No. 1, 2006

semiosis & causality

imprint-academic.com/C&HK